NOEL COWARD

DESIGN FOR LIVING

A Comedy in Three Acts

Garden City, New York

Doubleday, Doran and Company, Inc.

MCMXXXIII

ACT ONE

Otto's Studio in Paris.

ACT TWO

SCENE I—Leo's Flat in London. (*Eighteen months later.*)

SCENE II—The Same. (*A few days later.*)

SCENE III—The Same. (*The next morning.*)

ACT THREE

SCENE I—Ernest's Apartment in New York. (*Two years later.*)

SCENE II—The Same. (*The next morning.*)

TIME: The Present.

CHARACTERS

GILDA

OTTO

LEO

ERNEST FRIEDMAN

MISS HODGE

MR. BIRBECK

HENRY CARVER

HELEN CARVER

GRACE TORRENCE

MATTHEW

ACT ONE

ACT ONE: Scene I

THE SCENE *is rather a shabby studio in Paris. There is
a large window at the back looking out onto roof tops.
Down stage, on the Left, there is a door leading onto the
stairs, which in turn lead to the street. Up stage, on
the Right, there is a door leading into a small kitchen.*

*When the curtain rises, it is about ten o'clock on
a spring morning, and the studio is empty. GILDA
comes in from the kitchen carrying a coffee pot and a
milk jug. She places them on a table just under the
window, which is already laid with cups and plates,
etc. GILDA is a good-looking woman of about thirty.*

*Suddenly there is a knock on the door Left. She
gives a quick glance towards it, and then goes swiftly
and silently into the bedroom. In a moment she returns, closing the bedroom door carefully behind her.
There is another knock on the door. She opens it,
admitting ERNEST FRIEDMAN. He is any age between forty and fifty, rather precise in manner. He
carries a large package, obviously a picture, done up in
brown paper.*

GILDA: Ernest!
ERNEST: May I come in?
GILDA: I'd no idea you were back.
ERNEST: I arrived last night.
He comes in and puts down the package.

[*3*]

GILDA: What's that?

ERNEST: Something exquisite, superb.

GILDA: The Matisse?

ERNEST: Yes.

GILDA: You got it, after all.

ERNEST: It's unbelievable.

GILDA: Undo it quickly!

ERNEST: Otto must see it, too.

GILDA: He's asleep.

ERNEST: Wake him up, then.

GILDA: Not now, Ernest; he's had the most awful neuralgia all night.

ERNEST: Neuralgia?

GILDA: Yes; all up one side of his face and down the other side.

ERNEST (*undoing the package*): Wake him up. One look at this will take away his neuralgia immediately.

GILDA: No, really. He's only just dropped off. He's been in agony. I've dosed him with aspirin and given him a hot-water bottle here, and another one just there——

ERNEST (*petulantly*): I didn't know anyone had so many hot-water bottles.

GILDA: I still have one more, in case it spreads.

ERNEST: It really is very irritating. I take the trouble to drag this large picture all the way round here and Otto chooses to have neuralgia.

GILDA: He didn't choose to have it. He hated having it. His little face is all pinched and strained.

ERNEST: Otto's face is enormous.

GILDA: Show me the picture, Ernest, and try not to be disagreeable.

[4]

ERNEST (*grumbling*): It's an anticlimax.

GILDA: Thank you, dear.

ERNEST: It's no use pretending to be hurt. You know you don't really care for anybody's pictures except Otto's.

GILDA: Do you want some coffee?

ERNEST: Why are there two cups, if Otto has neuralgia?

GILDA: Habit.   There are always two cups.

ERNEST (*propping up the picture, facing up stage*): There!

GILDA (*scrutinizing it*): Yes, it's good.

ERNEST: Stand further back.

GILDA (*obliging*): Very good indeed.   How much?

ERNEST: Eight hundred pounds.

GILDA: Did you bargain?

ERNEST: No, that was their price.

GILDA: I think you were right.   Dealers or private owners?

ERNEST: Dealers.

GILDA: Here's your coffee.

ERNEST (*taking the cup and still looking at the picture*): It's strangely unlike all the other work, isn't it?

GILDA: What are you going to do with it?

ERNEST: Wait a little.

GILDA: And then resell?

ERNEST: I expect so.

GILDA: It will need a room to itself.

ERNEST: None of your decorating schemes. Hands off!

GILDA: Don't you think I'm a good decorator?

ERNEST: Not particularly.

GILDA: Darling Ernest!

ERNEST (*back at the picture*): Otto will go mad when he sees it.

GILDA: You think Otto's good, don't you? You think he's all right?

ERNEST: Coming along.   Coming along very nicely.

GILDA: Better than that.   Much better!

ERNEST: Lady Jaguar, defending her young!

GILDA: Otto isn't my young.

ERNEST: Oh, yes, he is.   Otto's everybody's young.

GILDA: You think he's weak, don't you?

ERNEST: Certainly, I do.

GILDA: And that I'm strong?

ERNEST: Strong as an ox!

GILDA: You've called me a jaguar and an ox within the last two minutes.   I wish you wouldn't be quite so zoological.

ERNEST: A temperamental ox, Gilda.   Sometimes a hysterical ox; and, at the moment, an over-vehement ox! What's the matter with you this morning?

GILDA: The matter with me?

ERNEST: There's a wild gleam in your eye.

GILDA: There always is.   It's one of my greatest charms!   I'm surprised that you never noticed it before.

ERNEST: The years are creeping on me, Gilda.   Perhaps my perceptions are getting dulled.

GILDA (*absently*): Perhaps they are.

ERNEST: If, in my dotage, I become a bore to you, you won't scruple to let me know, will you?

GILDA: Don't be an idiot!

ERNEST (*ruminatively*): Perhaps it was wrong of me to

[6]

arrive unexpectedly; I should have written you a little note making an appointment.

GILDA: Be a nice bluebottle and stop buzzing at me, will you?

ERNEST: You're a striking-looking woman—particularly when a little distrait.   It's a pity Otto's paintings of you have always been so tranquil.   He's missed something.

GILDA: The next time he paints me, you must be here to lash me with gay witticisms.

ERNEST: Surely, in my rôle of bitter old family friend, I can demand a little confidence!   You could tell me quite safely, you know, if anything's wrong.   I might even be able to help, with a senile word or two.

GILDA: Nothing is wrong, I tell you.

ERNEST: Nothing at all?

GILDA: Shall I make you some toast?

ERNEST: No, thank you.

GILDA: It's very hot today, isn't it?

ERNEST: Why not open the window?

GILDA: I never thought of it.

She opens the window almost violently.

There!—I'm sick of this studio; it's squalid!   I wish I were somewhere quite different.   I wish I were somebody quite different.   I wish I were a nice-minded British matron, with a husband, a cook, and a baby.   I wish I believed in God and the *Daily Mail* and "Mother India"!

ERNEST: I wish you'd tell me what's upsetting you.

GILDA: Glands, I expect.   Everything's glandular. I read a book about it the other day.   Ernest, if you only realized what was going on inside you, you'd be bitterly offended!

ERNEST: I'm much more interested in what's going on inside you.

GILDA: I'll tell you. All the hormones in my blood are working overtime. They're rushing madly in and out of my organs like messenger boys.

ERNEST: Why?

GILDA: Perhaps it's a sort of presentiment.

ERNEST: Psychic. I see. Well, well, well!

GILDA: Yes, I hear voices. I hear my own voice louder than any of the others, and it's beginning to bore me. Would you describe me as a super-egoist, Ernest?

ERNEST: Yes, dear.

GILDA: Thinking of myself too much, and not enough of other people?

ERNEST: No. Thinking of other people too much through yourself.

GILDA: How can anyone do otherwise?

ERNEST: Detachment of mind.

GILDA: I haven't got that sort of mind.

ERNEST: It's an acquired attitude and difficult to achieve, but, believe me, well worth trying for.

GILDA: Are you presenting yourself as a shining example?

ERNEST: Not shining, my dear, just dully effulgent.

GILDA: How should I start? Go away alone with my thoughts?

ERNEST: With all my detachment I find it very difficult to regard your painful twistings and turnings with composure.

GILDA: Why?

[*8*]

Ernest (*blandly*): Because I'm very fond of you.

Gilda: Why?

Ernest: I don't know. A tedious habit, I suppose. After all, I was very attached to your mother.

Gilda: Yes, I know. Personally, I never cared for her very much. A bossy woman.

Ernest: I don't think you should allude to the dead as "bossy."

Gilda: No reverence. That's my trouble. No reverence.

Ernest: I feel vaguely paternal towards you.

Gilda: Yes, Ernest.

Ernest: And your behaviour confuses me.

Gilda: My painful twistings and turnings.

Ernest: Exactly.

Gilda: What did you mean by that?

Ernest: Will you explain one thing to me really satisfactorily?

Gilda: What?

Ernest: Why don't you marry Otto?

Gilda: It's very funny that underneath all your worldly wisdom you're nothing but a respectable little old woman in a jet bonnet.

Ernest: You don't like being disapproved of, do you?

Gilda: Does anybody?

Ernest: Anyhow, I don't disapprove of you, yourself —of course, you're as obstinate as a mule——

Gilda: There you go again! "Strong as an ox!" "Obstinate as a mule!" Just a pack of Animal Grab— that's what I am! Bring out all the other cards. "Gentle as a dove!" "Playful as a kitten!" "Black as a crow!"——

Ernest: "Brave as a lion!"——

Gilda: Oh, no, Ernest! You couldn't think that, disapproving of me as you do.

Ernest: I was about to explain, when you so rudely interrupted, that it isn't you, yourself, I disapprove of. It's your mode of life.

Gilda (*laughing slightly*): Oh, I see!

Ernest: Your life is so dreadfully untidy, Gilda.

Gilda: I'm not a tidy person.

Ernest: You haven't yet answered my original question.

Gilda: Why I don't marry Otto?

Ernest: Yes. Is there a real reason, or just a lot of faintly affected theories?

Gilda: There's a very real reason.

Ernest: Well?

Gilda: I love him. (*She glances towards the bedroom door and says louder*): I love him.

Ernest: All right! All right, there's no need to shout.

Gilda: Yes, there is, every need. I should like to scream.

Ernest: That would surely be very bad for Otto's neuralgia.

Gilda (*calming down*): The only reasons for me to marry would be these: To have children; to have a home; to have a background for social activities, and to be provided for. Well, I don't like children; I don't wish for a home; I can't bear social activities, and I have a small but adequate income of my own. I love Otto deeply, and I respect him as a person and as an artist. To be tied legally to him would be repellent to me and to him, too. It's not a dashing bohemian gesture to Free

Love: we just feel like that, both of us. Now, are you satisfied?

ERNEST: If you are.

GILDA: You're impossible, Ernest. You sit there looking quizzical, and it maddens me!

ERNEST: I am quizzical.

GILDA: Well, be something else, for God's sake!

ERNEST: I suppose you know Leo is back?

GILDA (*jumping slightly*): What?

ERNEST: I said, "I suppose you know Leo is back?"

GILDA (*tremendously astonished*): It's not true!

ERNEST: Didn't he let you know?

GILDA (*eagerly*): When did he arrive? Where's he staying?

ERNEST: He arrived yesterday on the *Mauretania*. I had a note from him last night.

GILDA: Where's he staying?

ERNEST: You'll be shocked when I tell you.

GILDA: Quickly!—Quickly!

ERNEST: The George V.

GILDA (*going off into peals of laughter*): He must be raving! The George V! Oh, dear, oh, dear! Leo, at the George V! It's a glorious picture. Marble bathrooms and private balconies! Leo in all that grandeur! It isn't possible.

ERNEST: I gather he's made a good deal of money.

GILDA: That's not enough excuse. He ought to be ashamed of himself!

ERNEST: I can't understand him, not letting you know he was back. I fully expected to find him here.

GILDA: He'll appear sooner or later.

ERNEST: Are you glad he's made money?

GILDA: Why do you ask that?

ERNEST: Curiosity.

GILDA: Of course I'm glad. I adore Leo!

ERNEST: And Otto? What about Otto?

GILDA (*irritably*): What do you mean, "What about Otto?"

ERNEST: Will he be glad, too?

GILDA: You're too ridiculous sometimes, Ernest. What are you suspecting? What are you trying to find out?

ERNEST: Nothing. I was only wondering.

GILDA: It's all right. I know what you're getting at; but you're wrong as usual. Everybody's always wrong about Leo and Otto and me. I'm not jealous of Leo's money and success, and Otto won't be either when he knows. That's what you were suspecting, wasn't it?

ERNEST: Perhaps.

GILDA (*turning away*): I think you should grasp the situation a little better, having known us all for so long.

ERNEST: Otto and Leo knew each other first.

GILDA: Yes, yes, yes, yes—I know all about that! I came along and spoilt everything! Go on, dear——

ERNEST: I didn't say that.

GILDA (*sharply*): It's what you meant.

ERNEST: I think, perhaps, you may have spoilt yourself a little.

GILDA: Distrust of women frequently sets in at your age, Ernest.

ERNEST: I cannot, for the life of me, imagine why I'm so fond of you. You have such abominable manners.

GILDA: It's probably the scarlet life I live, causing me to degenerate into a shrew.

ERNEST: Very likely.

GILDA (*suddenly, leaning over the back of his chair, with her arms around him*): I'm sorry—about my bad manners, I mean. Please forgive me. You're a darling, and you love us a lot, don't you? All three of us? Me a little less than Otto and Leo because I'm a woman and, therefore, unreliable. Isn't that true?

ERNEST (*patting her hand*): Quite.

GILDA (*leaving him*): Your affection is a scared thing, though. Too frightened; too apprehensive of consequences. Leave us to grapple with the consequences, my dear. We're bound to have a bad time every now and then, but, at least, we know it. We're aware of a whole lot of things. Look at us clearly as human beings, rather peculiar human beings, I grant you, and don't be prejudiced by our lack of social grace. I laughed too loudly just now at the thought of Leo being rich and rare. Too loudly because I was uneasy, not jealous. I don't want him to be any different, that's all.

ERNEST: I see.

GILDA: Do you? Do you really? I doubt it. I don't see how anyone outside could. But I would like you to understand one thing absolutely and completely. I love Otto—whatever happens, I love Otto.

ERNEST: I never suggested for a moment that you didn't.

GILDA: Wait. Wait and see. The immediate horizon is grey and forbidding and dangerous. You don't know what I'm talking about and you probably think I've gone mad, and I can't explain—not now. But, darling Ernest, there's a crisis on. A full-blooded, emotional crisis; and when I need you, which I expect will be very soon, I shall yell! I shall yell like mad!

[*13*]

ERNEST: I knew you were in a state about something.

GILDA: Nasty shrewd little instincts shooting out and discovering things lurking in the atmosphere. It's funny about atmosphere, isn't it? Strong inside thoughts make outside impressions. Imprints on the ether. A horrid sort of spiritual television.

ERNEST: Quite.

GILDA: Well, are you satisfied now? You felt something was the matter, and you were right. It's always pleasant to be right, isn't it?

ERNEST: Not by any means.

GILDA: You're right about something else, too.

ERNEST: What?

GILDA: Women being unreliable. There are moments in life when I look upon my own damned femininity with complete nausea. There!

ERNEST (*smiling*): Good!

GILDA: I don't like women at all, Ernest; and I like myself least of any of them.

ERNEST: Never mind.

GILDA: I do mind. I mind bitterly. It humiliates me to the dust to think that I can go so far, clearly and intelligently, keeping faith with my own standards—which are not female standards at all—preserving a certain decent integrity, not using any tricks; then, suddenly, something happens, a spark is struck and down I go into the mud! Squirming with archness, being aloof and desirable, consciously alluring, snatching and grabbing, evading and surrendering, dressed and painted for victory. An object of strange contempt!

ERNEST: A lurid picture, perhaps a trifle exaggerated.

GILDA: I wish it were.   I wish it were
ERNEST: Drink a little coffee.
GILDA: Perhaps you're right.
   She sits down suddenly.
ERNEST (*pouring it out*): There!
GILDA: Thank you, Ernest.   You're a great comfort.
   She sips a little.
It's not very nice, is it?
ERNEST: Disgusting!
GILDA: I must have burnt it.
ERNEST: You did, dear.
GILDA: How lovely to be you!
ERNEST: In heaven's name, why?
GILDA: You're a permanent spectator.   You deal in
pictures.   You look at pictures all day long, good pic-
tures and bad pictures; gay pictures and gloomy pictures,
and you know why they're this or why they're that,
because you're critical and knowledgeable and wise.
You're a clever little dear, that's what you are—a clever
little dear!
   She begins to laugh again.
ERNEST: Gilda, stop it!
GILDA: Take a look at this, my darling.   Measure it
with your eyes.   Portrait of a woman in three cardinal
colours.   Portrait of a too loving spirit tied down to a
predatory feminine carcass.
ERNEST: This is definitely macabre.
GILDA: Right, again!
ERNEST: I think I'd better go.   You ought to lie down
or something.
   GILDA (*hysterically*): Stay a little longer, you'll find
out so much.

ERNEST: I don't want to find out anything. You're scaring me to death.

GILDA: Courage, Ernest. Be brave. Look at the whole thing as a side show. People pay to see freaks. Walk up! Walk up and see the Fat Lady and the Monkey Man and the Living Skeleton and the Three Famous Hermaphrodites!——

There is a noise outside in the passage. The door bursts open, and OTTO *fairly bounds into the room. He is tall and good-looking, wearing a travelling coat and hat, and carrying a suitcase and a large package of painting materials.*

GILDA: Otto!

OTTO (*striking an attitude*): I've come home!

GILDA: You see what happens when I crack the whip!

OTTO: Little Ernest! How very sweet to see you!

He kisses him.

GILDA: When did you leave Bordeaux?

OTTO: Night train, dear heart.

GILDA: Why didn't you telegraph?

OTTO: I don't hold with these modern innovations.

ERNEST: This is very interesting.

OTTO: What's very interesting?

ERNEST: Life, Otto. I was just meditating upon Life.

OTTO (*to* GILDA): I've finished the picture.

GILDA: Really? Completely finished it?

OTTO: Yes, it's fine. I brought it away with me. I made the old fool sit for hours and wouldn't let her see, and afterwards when she did she made the most awful scene. She said it was out of drawing and made her look podgy; then I lost my temper and said it was overeating and lack of exercise that made her look podgy, and that it was not only an exquisite painting but unfalteringly true to life. Then she practically ordered me out of the house! I don't suppose she'll ever pay me the rest of the money, but to hell with her! If she doesn't, I shall have the picture.

ERNEST: Unwise, but, I am sure, enjoyable.

There is silence.

OTTO: Well?

GILDA: Well what?

OTTO: What on earth's the matter?

GILDA: Why should you think anything's the matter?

OTTO (*looking from one to the other*): Have your faces lit up? No. Have you rushed at me with outstretched arms? No. Are you, either of you, even remotely pleased to see me? Obviously NO! Something dreadful has happened and you're trying to decide how to break the news to me. What is it? Tell me at once! What's the matter?

ERNEST (*with slight malice*): Gilda has neuralgia.

OTTO: Nonsense! She's as strong as a horse.

GILDA (*laughing wildly*): Oh, my God!

OTTO (*to* ERNEST): What's she "Oh, my God-ing" about?

ERNEST: It's glandular. Everything's glandular.

OTTO: Have you both gone mad?

GILDA: Don't take off your coat and hat.

OTTO: What?

GILDA (*very slowly and distinctly*): I said, "Don't take off your coat and hat."

OTTO (*humouring her*): Very well, darling, I won't, I promise you. As a matter of fact, I said to myself only

[*17*]

this morning, "Otto," I said, "Otto, you must never, never be parted from your coat and hat! Never, never, never!"

GILDA: There's a surprise for you, darling. A beautiful surprise!

OTTO: What?

GILDA: You must go to the George V at once.

OTTO: The George V?

GILDA: Yes. That's the surprise.

OTTO: Who is it? Who's at the George V?

GILDA: Leo.

OTTO: You're not serious? He couldn't be.

GILDA: He is. He came back on the *Mauretania*. His play is still running in Chicago, and he's sold the movie rights and he's made thousands!

OTTO: Have you seen him?

GILDA: Of course! Last night.

ERNEST: Well, I'm damned!

GILDA: I told you you didn't understand, Ernest. (*To* OTTO): If you'd only let me know you were coming, we could have both met you at the station. It would have been so lovely! Leo will be furious. You must go to him at once and bring him back here and we'll make some sort of a plan for the day.

OTTO: This is good, good, better than good! An excellent, super homecoming! I was thinking of him last night, bumping along in that awful train. I thought of him for hours, I swear I did. Cross my hand with silver, lady, I'm so definitely the Gipsy Queen! Oh, God, how marvellous! He'll be able to go to Annecy with us.

GILDA: He's got to go back to New York, and then to London,

[*18*]

Otto: Splendid! We'll go with him. He's been away far too long. Come on——

He seizes Gilda's *hand.*

Gilda: No.

Ernest: What are you going to do?

Gilda: Stay here and tidy up. You go with Otto to fetch Leo. You said my life was untidy, didn't you? Well, I'm taking it to heart!

Otto: Come on, Gilda; it doesn't matter about tidying up.

Gilda: Yes, it does. It does! It's the most important thing in the world—an orderly mind; that's the thing to have.

Otto: He's probably brought us presents, and if he's rich they'll be expensive presents. Very nice! Very nice, indeed. Come along, Ernest, my little honey— we'll take a taxi.

Ernest: I don't think I'll go.

Otto: You must. He likes seeing you almost as much as us. Come on!

He grabs Ernest *by the shoulders and shoves him towards the door.*

Gilda: Of course, go, Ernest, and come back too and we'll all celebrate. I'm yelling! Can't you hear me yelling like mad?

Otto: What on earth are you talking about?

Gilda: A bad joke, and very difficult to explain.

Otto: Good-morning, darling! I never kissed you good-morning.

Gilda: Never mind about that now. Go on, both of you, or he'll have gone out. You don't want to miss him.

OTTO (*firmly kissing her*): Good-morning, darling.

GILDA (*suddenly stiffening in his arms*): Dearest——

    OTTO *and* ERNEST *go to the door.*

GILDA (*suddenly*): Otto——!

OTTO (*turning*): Yes?

GILDA (*smiling gaily, but with a slight strain in her voice*): I love you very much, so be careful crossing roads, won't you? Look to the right and the left and all around everything, and don't do anything foolish and impulsive. Please remember, there's a dear——

OTTO: Be quiet, don't pester me with your attentions! (*To* ERNEST *as they go out*): She's crazy about me, poor little thing; just crazy about me.

    They go out. GILDA *stands quite still for a moment or two staring after them; then she sits down at a table.* LEO *comes out of the bedroom.* He *is thin and nervous and obviously making a tremendous effort to control himself. He walks about aimlessly for a little and finishes up looking out of the window, with his back to* GILDA.

LEO: What now?

GILDA: I don't know.

LEO: Not much time to think.

GILDA: A few minutes.

LEO: Are there any cigarettes?

GILDA: Yes, in that box.

LEO: Want one?

GILDA: No.

LEO (*lighting one*): It's nice being human beings, isn't it? I'm sure God's angels must envy us.

GILDA: Whom do you love best? Otto or me?

LEO: Silly question.

Gilda: Answer me, anyhow.

Leo: How can I? Be sensible! In any case, what does it matter?

Gilda: It's important to me.

Leo: No, it isn't—not really. That's not what's important. What we did was inevitable. It's been inevitable for years. It doesn't matter who loves who the most; you can't line up things like that mathematically. We all love each other a lot, far too much, and we've made a bloody mess of it! That was inevitable, too.

Gilda: We must get it straight, somehow.

Leo: Yes, we must get it straight and tie it up with ribbons with a bow on the top. Pity it isn't Valentine's Day!

Gilda: Can't we laugh a little? Isn't it a joke? Can't we make it a joke?

Leo: Yes, it's a joke. It's a joke, all right. We can laugh until our sides ache. Let's start, shall we?

Gilda: What's the truth of it? The absolute, deep-down truth? Until we really know that, we can't grapple with it. We can't do a thing. We can only sit here flicking words about.

Leo: It should be easy, you know. The actual facts are so simple. I love you. You love me. You love Otto. I love Otto. Otto loves you. Otto loves me. There now! Start to unravel from there.

Gilda: We've always been honest, though, all of us. Honest with each other, I mean. That's something to go on, isn't it?

Leo: In this particular instance, it makes the whole thing far more complicated. If we were ordinary moral, high-thinking citizens we could carry on a backstairs affair for weeks without saying a word about it. We could lunch and dine together, all three, and not give anything away by so much as a look.

GILDA: If we were ordinary moral, high-thinking citizens we shouldn't have had an affair at all.

LEO: Perhaps not. We should have crushed it down. And the more we crushed it down the more we should have resented Otto, until we hated him. Just think of hating Otto——

GILDA: Just think of him hating us.

LEO: Do you think he will?

GILDA (*inexorably*): Yes.

LEO (*walking about the room*): Oh, no, no—he mustn't! It's too silly. He must see how unimportant it is, really.

GILDA: There's no question of not telling him, is there?

LEO: Of course not.

GILDA: We could pretend that you just arrived here and missed them on the way.

LEO: So we could, dear—so we could.

GILDA: Do you think we're working each other up? Do you think we're imagining it to be more serious than it really is?

LEO: Perhaps.

GILDA: Do you think, after all, he may not mind quite so dreadfully?

LEO: He'll mind just as much as you or I would under similar circumstances. Probably a little bit more. Imagine that for a moment, will you? Put yourself in his place.

GILDA (*hopelessly*): Oh, don't!

Leo: Tell me one thing. How sorry were you last night, when once you realized we were in for it?

Gilda: I wasn't sorry at all. I gave way utterly.

Leo: So did I.

Gilda: Very deep inside, I had a qualm or two. Just once or twice.

Leo: So did I.

Gilda: But I stamped on them, like killing beetles.

Leo: A nice way to describe the pangs of a noble conscience!

Gilda: I enjoyed it all, see! I enjoyed it thoroughly from the very first moment. So there!

Leo: All right! All right! So did I.

Gilda (*defiantly*): It was romantic. Suddenly, violently romantic! The whole evening was "Gala." You looked lovely, darling—very smooth and velvety—and your manner was a dream! I'd forgotten about your French accent and the way you move your hands, and the way you dance. A sleek little gigolo!

Leo: You must try not to be bitter, dear.

Gilda: There seemed to be something new about you: something I'd never realized before. Perhaps it's having money. Perhaps your success has given you a little extra glamour.

Leo: Look at me now, sweet! It's quite chilly, this morning light. How do I appear to you now?

Gilda (*gently*): The same.

Leo: So do you, but that's because my eyes are slow at changing visions. I still see you too clearly last night to be able to realize how you look this morning. You were very got up—very got up, indeed, in your green dress and your earrings. It was "Gala," all right—strong magic!

[*23*]

GILDA: Coloured lights, sly music, overhanging trees, paper streamers—all the trappings.

LEO: Champagne, too, just to celebrate, both of us hating it.

GILDA: We drank to Otto. Perhaps you remember that as well?

LEO: Perfectly.

GILDA: How could we? Oh, how could we?

LEO: It seemed quite natural.

GILDA: Yes, but we knew in our hearts what we were up to. It was vile of us.

LEO: I'll drink Otto's health until the day I die! Nothing could change that ever.

GILDA: Sentimentalist!

LEO: Deeper than sentiment: far, far deeper. Beyond the reach of small enchantments.

GILDA: Was that all it was to you? A small enchantment?

LEO: That's all it ever is to anybody, if only they knew.

GILDA: Easy wisdom. Is it a comfort to you?

LEO: Not particularly.

GILDA (*viciously*): Let's have some more! "Passion's only transitory," isn't it? "Love is ever fleeting!" "Time is a great healer." Trot them all out, dear.

LEO: Don't try to quarrel with me.

GILDA: Don't be so wise and assured and knowing, then. It's infuriating.

LEO: I believe I was more to blame than you, really.

GILDA: Why?

LEO: I made the running.

GILDA: *You* made the running!

　　She laughs.

[24]

Leo: A silly pride made me show off to you, parade my attraction for you, like a mannequin. New spring model, with a few extra flounces!

Gilda: That's my story, Leo; you can't steal it from me. I've been wallowing in self-abasement, dragging out my last night's femininity and spitting on it. I've taken the blame onto myself for the whole thing. Ernest was quite shocked; you should have been listening at the door.

Leo: I was.

Gilda: Good! Then you know how I feel.

Leo: Lot of damned hysteria.

Gilda: Possibly, but heartfelt at the moment.

Leo: Can't we put an end to this flagellation party now?

Gilda: We might just as well go on with it, it passes the time.

Leo: Until Otto comes back.

Gilda: Yes. Until Otto comes back.

Leo (*walking up and down*): I expect jealousy had something to do with it, too.

Gilda: Jealousy?

Leo: Yes. Subconscious and buried deep, but there all the same; there for ages, ever since our first meeting when you chose Otto so firmly.

Gilda: Another of those pleasant little galas! The awakening of spring! Romance in a café! Yes, sir! "Yes, sir, three bags full!"

Leo: A strange evening. Very gay, if I remember rightly.

Gilda: Oh, it was gay, deliriously gay, thick with omens!

Leo: Perhaps we laughed at them too hard.

Gilda: You and Otto had a row afterwards, didn't you?

Leo: Yes, a beauty.

Gilda: Blows?

Leo: Ineffectual blows. Otto fell into the bath!

Gilda: Was there any water in it?

Leo: Not at first.

Gilda (*beginning to laugh*): Leo, you didn't——?

Leo (*also beginning to laugh*): Of course I did; it was the obvious thing to do.

Gilda: Couldn't he get out?

Leo: Every time he tried, I pushed him back.

Gilda (*now laughing helplessly*): Oh, the poor darling!——

Leo (*giving way*): Finally—he—he got wedged——

Gilda: This is hysteria!   Stop it, stop it——

Leo (*sinking down at the table with his head in his hands, roaring with laughter*): It—it was a very narrow bath, far—far—too narrow——

Gilda (*collapsing at the other side of the table*): Shut up, for heaven's sake!   Shut up——

> *They are sitting there, groaning with laughter, when* Otto *comes into the room.*

Otto: Leo!

> *They both look up, and the laughter dies away from their faces.* Leo *rises and comes slowly over to* Otto. *He takes both his hands and stands looking at him.*

Leo: Hello, Otto.

Otto: Why did you stop laughing so suddenly?

Leo: It's funny how lovely it is to see you.

Otto: Why funny?

[*26*]

GILDA: Where's Ernest?

OTTO: He wouldn't come back with me. He darted off in a taxi very abruptly when we found Leo wasn't at the hotel. He seemed to be in a fluster.

LEO: Ernest's often in a fluster. It's part of his personality, I think.

OTTO: Ernest hasn't got a personality.

GILDA: Yes, he has; but it's only a very little one, gentle and prim.

OTTO: You've changed, Leo. Your face looks different.

LEO: In what way different?

OTTO: I don't know, sort of odd.

LEO: I was very seasick on the *Mauretania*. Perhaps that changed it.

GILDA: They call the *Mauretania* "The Greyhound of the Ocean." I wonder why?

LEO: Because it's too long and too thin and leaps up and down.

GILDA: Personally, I prefer the *Olympic*. It's a good-natured boat and cozy, also it has a Turkish bath.

LEO: I dearly love a Turkish bath.

OTTO: Have you both gone crazy?

LEO: Yes. Just for a little.

OTTO: What does that mean?

GILDA: Lots of things, Otto. Everything's quite horrid.

OTTO: I'm awfully puzzled. I wish you'd both stop hinting and tell me what's happened.

LEO: It's serious, Otto. Please try to be wise about it.

OTTO (*with slight irritation*): How the hell can I be wise about it if I don't know what it is?

[*27*]

LEO (*turning away*): Oh, God!   This is unbearable!

OTTO (*fighting against the truth that's dawning on him*): It wouldn't be what I think it is, would it?   I mean, what's just dropped into my mind.   It isn't that, is it?

GILDA: Yes.

LEO: Yes.

OTTO (*very quietly*): Oh, I see.

GILDA (*miserably*): If only you wouldn't look like that.

OTTO: I can't see that it matters very much how I look.

LEO: We're—we're both equally to blame.

OTTO: When did you arrive?   When—when did— don't you think you'd better tell me a little more?

LEO (*swiftly*): I arrived yesterday afternoon, and the moment I'd left my bags at the hotel I came straight here, naturally.   Gilda and I dined together, and I spent the night here.

OTTO: Oh—oh, did you?

LEO (*after a long pause*): Yes, I did.

OTTO: This is the second bad entrance I've made this morning.   I don't think I'd better make any more.

GILDA: Otto—darling—please, listen a minute!

OTTO: What is there to listen to?   What is there for you to say?

GILDA: Nothing.   You're quite right.   Nothing at all.

OTTO: Have you planned it?   Before, I mean?

LEO: Of course not.

OTTO: Was it in your minds?

LEO: Yes.   It's been in all our minds, for ages.   You know that.

OTTO: You couldn't have controlled yourself?   Not for my sake, alone, but for all that lies between us?

LEO: We could have, I suppose. But we didn't.

OTTO (*still quiet, but trembling*): Instead of meanly taking advantage of my being away, couldn't you have waited until I came back, and told me how you felt?

LEO: Would that have made things any better?

OTTO: It would have been honest, at least.

LEO (*with sudden violence*): Bunk! We're being as honest as we know how! Chance caught us, as it was bound to catch us eventually. We were doomed to it from the very first moment. You don't suppose we enjoy telling you, do you? You don't suppose I like watching the pleasure at seeing me fade out of your eyes? If it wasn't that we loved you deeply, both of us, we'd lie to you and deceive you indefinitely, rather than inflict this horror on ourselves.

OTTO (*his voice rising slightly*): And what about the horror you're inflicting on me?

GILDA: Don't argue, Leo. What's the use of arguing?

OTTO: So, you love me, do you? Both of you love me deeply! I don't want a love that can shut me out and make me feel more utterly alone than I've ever felt in my life before.

GILDA: Don't say that—it's not true! You couldn't be shut out—ever! Not possibly. Hold on to reason for a moment, for the sake of all of us—hold on to reason! It's our only chance. We've known this might happen any day; we've actually discussed it, quite calmly and rationally, but then there wasn't any emotion mixed up with it. Now there is, and we've got to fight it. It's distorting and overbalancing everything—don't you see? Oh, please, please try to see——

OTTO: I see all right.   Believe me, I see perfectly!

GILDA: You don't, really—it's hopeless.

OTTO: Quite hopeless.

GILDA: It needn't be, if only we can tide over this moment.

OTTO: Why should we tide over this moment?   It's a big moment!   Let's make the most of it.

He gives a little laugh.

LEO: I suppose that way of taking it is as good as any.

GILDA: No, it isn't—it isn't.

OTTO: I still find the whole thing a little difficult to realize completely.   You must forgive me for being so stupid.   I see quite clearly; I hear quite clearly; I know what's happened quite clearly, but I still don't quite understand.

LEO: What more do you want to understand?

OTTO: Were you both drunk?

GILDA: Of course we weren't.

OTTO: Then that's ruled out.   One thing is still bewildering me very much.   Quite a small trivial thing. You are both obviously strained and upset and unhappy at having to tell me.   Isn't that so?

GILDA: Yes.

OTTO: Then why were you laughing when I came in?

LEO: Oh, what on earth does that matter?

OTTO: It matters a lot.   It's very interesting.

LEO: It was completely irrelevant. Hysteria. It had nothing to do with anything.

OTTO: Why were you both laughing when I came in?

LEO: It was hysteria, I tell you.

OTTO: Were you laughing at me?

LEO (*wildly*): Yes, we were!   We were!   We were

laughing at you being wedged in the bath. That's what we were laughing at.

GILDA: Shut up, Leo! Stop it.

LEO (*giving way*): And I shall laugh at that until the end of my days—I shall roll about on my death bed thinking about it—and there are other things I shall laugh at, too. I shall laugh at you now, in this situation, being hurt and grieved and immeasurably calm. What right have you to be hurt and grieved, any more than Gilda and me? We're having just as bad a time as you are, probably worse. I didn't stamp about with a martyr's crown on when you rushed off with her, in the first place; I didn't look wistful and say I was shut out. And I don't intend to stand any of that nonsense from you! What happened between Gilda and me last night is actually completely unimportant—a sudden flare-up—and although we've been mutually attracted to each other for years, it wasn't even based on deep sexual love! It was just an unpremeditated roll in the hay and we enjoyed it very much, so there!

OTTO (*furiously*): Well, one thing that magnificent outburst has done for me is this: I don't feel shut out any more. Do you hear? Not any more! And I'm extremely grateful to you. You were right about me being hurt and grieved. I was. But that's over, too. I've seen something in you that I've never seen before; in all these years I've never noticed it—I never realized that, deep down underneath your superficial charm and wit, you're nothing but a cheap, second-rate little opportunist, ready to sacrifice anything, however sacred, to the excitement of the moment——

GILDA: Otto! Otto—listen a minute; please listen——

[*31*]

OTTO (*turning to her*): Listen to what? A few garbled explanations and excuses, fully charged with a hundred-per-cent feminine emotionalism, appealing to me to hold on to reason and intelligence as it's "our only chance." I don't want an "only chance"—I don't want a chance to do anything but say what I have to say and leave you both to your own god-damned devices! Where was this much vaunted reason and intelligence last night? Working overtime, I'm sure. Working in a hundred small female ways. I expect your reason and intelligence prompted you to wear your green dress, didn't it? With the emerald earrings? And your green shoes, too, although they hurt you when you dance. Reason must have whispered kindly in your ear on your way back here in the taxi. It must have said, "Otto's in Bordeaux, and Bordeaux is a long way away, so everything will be quite safe!" That's reason, all right—pure reason——

GILDA (*collapsing at the table*): Stop it! Stop it! How can you be so cruel! How can you say such vile things?

OTTO (*without a break*): I hope "intelligence" gave you a little extra jab and suggested that you lock the door? In furtive, underhand affairs doors are always locked——

LEO: Shut up, Otto. What's the use of going on like that?

OTTO: Don't speak to me—old, old Loyal Friend that you are! Don't speak to me, even if you have the courage, and keep out of my sight from now onwards——

LEO: Bravo, Deathless Drama!

OTTO: Wrong again. Lifeless Comedy. You've set me free from a stale affection that must have died ages ago without my realizing it. Go ahead, my boy, and do

[*32*]

great things! You've already achieved a Hotel de Luxe, a few smart suits, and the woman I loved. Go ahead, maybe there are still higher peaks for you to climb. Good luck, both of you! Wonderful luck! I wish you were dead and in hell!

He slams out of the room as the curtain falls.

END OF ACT ONE

ACT TWO

Scene I

ACT TWO: Scene I

THE SCENE *is* LEO's *flat in London. It is only a rented flat but very comfortably furnished. Two French windows at the back open onto a small balcony, which, in turn, overlooks a square. It is several floors up, so only the tops of trees can be seen; these are brown and losing their leaves, as it is autumn. Down stage, on the Right, are double doors leading to the hall. Above these, a small door leads to the kitchen. On the Left, up stage, another door leads to the bedroom and bathroom. There is a large picture of* GILDA, *painted by* OTTO, *hanging on the wall. The furniture may be left to the producer's discrimination.*

DISCOVERED: *When the curtain rises, it is about ten-thirty in the morning. Eighteen months have passed since Act One. The room is strewn with newspapers.* GILDA *is lying on the sofa, reading one;* LEO *is lying face downwards on the floor, reading another one.*

LEO (*rolling over on his back and flinging the paper in the air*): It's a knockout! It's magnificent! It'll run a year.

GILDA: Two years.

LEO: Three years.

GILDA: Four years, five years, six years! It'll run for ever. Old ladies will be trampled to death struggling

[*37*]

to get into the pit. Women will have babies regularly in the upper circle bar during the big scene at the end of the second act——

LEO (*complacently*): Regularly as clockwork.

GILDA: The *Daily Mail* says it's daring and dramatic and witty.

LEO: The *Daily Express* says it's disgusting.

GILDA: I should be cut to the quick if it said anything else.

LEO: The *Daily Mirror*, I regret to say, is a trifle carping.

GILDA: Getting uppish, I see. Naughty little thing!

LEO (*reading the* Daily Mirror): "*Change and Decay* is gripping throughout. The characterization falters here and there, but the dialogue is polished and sustains a high level from first to last and is frequently witty, nay, even brilliant——"

GILDA: I love "Nay."

LEO (*still reading*): "But"—here we go, dear!—"But the play, on the whole, is decidedly thin."

GILDA: My God! They've noticed it.

LEO (*jumping up*): Thin—thin! What do they mean "thin"?

GILDA: Just thin, darling. Thin's thin all the world over and you can't get away from it.

LEO: Would you call it thin?

GILDA: Emaciated.

LEO: I shall write fat plays from now onwards. Fat plays filled with very fat people!

GILDA: You mustn't let your vibrations be upset by the *Daily Mirror*. It means to be kind. That's why one only looks at the pictures.

[*38*]

Leo: The *Daily Sketch* is just as bad.

Gilda (*gently*): Just as good, dear—just as good.

Leo: Let's have another look at Old Father *Times*.

Gilda: It's there, behind the *Telegraph*.

Leo (*glancing through it*): Noncommittal, but amiable. A minute, if slightly inaccurate, description of the plot.

Gilda (*rising and looking over his shoulder*): Only a few of the names wrong.

Leo: They seem to have missed the main idea of the play.

Gilda: You mustn't grumble; they say the lines are provocative.

Leo: What *could* they mean by that?

Gilda: Anyhow, you can't expect a paper like the *Times* to be really interested in your petty little excursions in the theatre. After all, it is the organ of the nation.

Leo: That sounds vaguely pornographic to me.

The telephone rings.

Leo (*answering it*): Hallow! Hallow—'oo is it speaking?—H'if—if you will kaindly 'old the line for a moment, h'I will ascertain.

He places his hand over the receiver.

Lady Brevell!

Gilda: Tell her to go to hell.

Leo: It's the third time she's rung up this morning.

Gilda: No restraint. That's what's wrong with Society nowadays.

Leo (*at telephone again*): Hallow, hallow!—I am seu very sorry but Mr. Mercuré is not awake yet. 'E 'ad a very tiring night what with one thing and another. H'is there any message?—Lunch on the third—or dinner on

the seventh.—Yes, I'll write it daown—not at all!—
Thenk you.

Gilda (*seriously*): How do you feel about all that?

Leo: Amused.

Gilda: I'm not sure that I do.

Leo: It's only funny, really.

Gilda: Yes, but dangerous.

Leo: Are you frightened that my silly fluffy little
head will be turned?

Gilda: No, not exactly, but it makes me uncomfortable, this snatching that goes on.   Success is far more
perilous than failure, isn't it?   You've got to be doubly
strong and watchful and wary.

Leo: Perhaps I shall survive.

Gilda: You'll survive all right, in the long run—I
don't doubt that for a moment.   It's me I was worrying
about.

Leo: Why?

Gilda: Not me, alone.   Us.

Leo: Oh, I see.

Gilda: Maybe I'm jealous of you.   I never thought
of that.

Leo: Darling, don't be silly!

Gilda: Last year was bad enough.   This is going to
be far worse.

Leo: Why be scared?

Gilda: Where do we go from here?   That's what I
want to know.

Leo: How would you feel about getting married?

Gilda (*laughing*): It's not that, dear!

Leo: I know it isn't, but——

Gilda: But what?

LEO: It might be rather fun. We'd get a lot more presents now than if we'd done it before.

GILDA: A very grand marriage. St. Margaret's, Westminster?

LEO: Yes, with a tremendous "do" at Claridge's afterwards.

GILDA: The honeymoon would be thrilling, wouldn't it? Just you and me, alone, finding out about each other.

LEO: I'd be very gentle with you, very tender.

GILDA: You'd get a sock in the jaw, if you were!

LEO (*shocked*): Oh, how volgar! How inexpressibly volgar!

GILDA: It's an enjoyable idea to play with, isn't it?

LEO: Let's do it.

GILDA: Stop! Stop, stop—you're rushing me off my feet!

LEO: No, but seriously, it's a much better plan than you think. It would ease small social situations enormously. The more successful I become, the more complicated everything's going to get. Let's do it, Gilda.

GILDA: No.

LEO: Why not?

GILDA: It wouldn't do. Really, it wouldn't.

LEO: I think you're wrong.

GILDA: It doesn't matter enough about the small social situations, those don't concern me much, anyway. They never have and they never will. I shouldn't feel cozy, married! It would upset my moral principles.

LEO: Doesn't the Eye of Heaven mean anything to you?

GILDA: Only when it winks!

[*41*]

LEO: God knows, it ought to wink enough at our marriage.

GILDA: Also, there's another thing.

LEO: What?

GILDA: Otto.

LEO: Otto!

GILDA: Yes. I think he'd hate it.

LEO: I wonder if he would.

GILDA: I believe so. There'd be no reason for him to, really; but I believe he would.

LEO: If only he'd appear again we could ask him.

GILDA: He will, sooner or later; he can't go on being cross for ever.

LEO: Funny, about Otto.

GILDA: Screamingly funny.

LEO: Do you love him still?

GILDA: Of course. Don't you?

LEO (*sighing*): Yes.

GILDA: We couldn't *not* love Otto, really.

LEO: Could you live with him again?

GILDA: No, I don't think so; that part of it's dead.

LEO: We were right, weren't we? Unconditionally right.

GILDA: Yes. I wish it hadn't been so drastic, though, and violent and horrid. I hated him being made so unhappy.

LEO: We weren't any too joyful ourselves, at first.

GILDA: Conscience gnawing at our vitals.

LEO: Do you think—do you think he'll ever get over it, enough for us all to be together again?

GILDA (*with sudden vehemence*): I don't want all to be together again.

The telephone rings.

LEO: Damn!

GILDA (*humming*): Oh, Death, where is thy sting-a-ling-a-ling——

LEO (*at telephone*): Hallow! Hallow—Neo, I'm afraid he's eout.

He hangs up.

GILDA: Why don't you let Miss Hodge answer the telephone? It would save you an awful lot of trouble.

LEO: Do you think she could?

GILDA: I don't see why not; she seems in full possession of most of her faculties.

LEO: Where is she?

GILDA: She's what's known as "doing the bedroom."

LEO (*calling*): Miss Hodge—Miss Hodge——

GILDA: We ought to have a valet in a white coat, really. Think if television came in suddenly, and everyone who rang up was faced with Miss Hodge!

MISS HODGE *enters.* *She is dusty and extremely untidy.*

MISS HODGE: Did you call?

LEO: Yes, Miss Hodge.

MISS HODGE: I was doing the bedroom.

LEO: Yes, I know you were and I'm sorry to disturb you, but I have a favour to ask you.

MISS HODGE (*suspiciously*): Favour?

LEO: Yes. Every time the telephone rings, will you answer it for me?

MISS HODGE (*with dignity*): If I 'appen to be where I can 'ear it, I will with pleasure.

LEO: Thank you very much. Just ask who it is speaking and tell them to hold the line.

[*43*]

MISS HODGE: 'Ow long for?

LEO: Until you've told me.

MISS HODGE: All right.

She goes back into the bedroom.

LEO: I fear no good will come of that.

GILDA: Do you think while I am here alone in the evenings, when you are rushing madly from party to party, I might find out about Miss Hodge's inner life?

The telephone rings.

LEO: There now!

They both wait while the telephone continues to ring.

GILDA (*sadly*): Two valets in two white coats, that's what we need, and a secretary and an upper house-maid!

The telephone continues to ring.

LEO: Perhaps I'd better answer it, after all.

GILDA: No, let it ring.   I love the tone.

MISS HODGE *comes flying in breathlessly, and rushes to the telephone.*

MISS HODGE (*at telephone*): 'Allo! 'Allo! 'Allo-'allo-'allo-'allo!——

GILDA: This is getting monotonous.

MISS HODGE (*continuing*): 'Allo, 'allo—'allo! 'Allo——

GILDA (*conversationally*): Tell me, Mr. Mercuré, what do you think of the modern girl?

LEO (*politely*): A silly bitch.

GILDA: How cynical!

MISS HODGE: . . . 'allo, 'allo, 'allo, 'allo—'Allo! 'Allo——

She turns to them despondently.

There don't seem to be anyone there.

LEO: Never mind, Miss Hodge. We mustn't hope for too much, at first. Thank you very much.

MISS HODGE: Not at all, sir.

She goes out again.

GILDA: I feel suddenly irritated.

LEO: Why?

GILDA: I don't know. Reaction, I expect, after the anxiety of the last few days. Now it's all over and everything seems rather blank. How happy are you, really?

LEO: Very, I think.

GILDA: I don't work hard enough, not nearly hard enough; I've only done four houses for four silly women since we've been in England.

LEO: Monica Jevon wants you to do hers the moment she comes back.

GILDA: That'll make the fifth silly woman.

LEO: She's not so particularly silly.

GILDA: She's nice, really, nicer than most of them, I suppose. Oh, dear!

LEO: Cigarette?

He throws her one.

GILDA: Ernest was right.

LEO: How do you mean? When?

GILDA: Ages ago. He said my life was untidy. And it is untidy. At this moment it's untidier than ever. Perhaps you're wise about our marrying; perhaps it would be a good thing. I'm developing into one of those tedious unoccupied women, who batten on men and spoil everything for them. I'm spoiling the excitement of your success for you now by being tiresome and gloomy.

LEO: Do you think marriage would automatically

[45]

transform you into a busy, high-spirited Peg-o'-My-Heart?

GILDA: Something's missing, and I don't know what it is.

LEO: Don't you?

GILDA: No. Do you?

LEO: Yes, I do. I know perfectly well what's missing——

The telephone rings again.

GILDA: I'll do it this time.

She goes to the telephone.

Hallo! Yes.—Oh, yes, of course! How do you do?—Yes, he's here, I'll call him.—What?—I'm sure he'd love to.—That's terribly sweet of you, but I'm afraid I can't.—No, I've got to go to Paris.—No, only for a few days.

LEO: Who is it?

GILDA (*with her hand over the receiver*): Mrs. Borrowdale. She wants you for the week-end.—(*Into telephone again*): Here he is.

LEO (*taking telephone*): Hallo, Marion.—Yes, wasn't it marvellous?—Terrified out of my seven senses.—What?—Well, I'm not sure——

GILDA (*hissing at him*): Yes, you are—quite sure!

LEO: Just hold on one minute while I look at my book.—

He puts his hand over the receiver.

What will you do if I go?

GILDA: Commit suicide immediately, don't be so silly——

LEO: Why didn't you accept, too? She asked you.

GILDA: Because I don't want to go.

[*46*]

Leo (*at telephone*): No, there isn't a thing down for Saturday. I'd love to come.—Yes, that'll be grand.—Good-bye.

He comes over to Gilda.

Why don't you want to come? She's awfully amusing, and the house is lovely.

Gilda: It's much better for you to go alone.

Leo: All right. Have it your own way.

Gilda: Don't think I'm being tiresome again, there's a darling! I just couldn't make the effort—that's the honest-to-God reason. I'm no good at house parties; I never was.

Leo: Marion's house parties are different. You can do what you like and nobody worries you.

Gilda: I can never find what I like in other people's houses, and everybody worries me.

Leo: I suppose I must be more gregarious than you. I enjoy meeting new people.

Gilda: I enjoy meeting new people, too, but not second-hand ones.

Leo: As I said before, Marion's house parties are extremely amusing. She doesn't like "second-hand" people, as you call them, any more than you do. Incidentally, she's a very intelligent woman herself and exceedingly good company.

Gilda: I never said she wasn't intelligent, and I'm sure she's excellent company. She has to be. It's her job.

Leo: That was a cheap gibe—thoroughly cheap——

The telephone rings again. Miss Hodge *surprisingly appears almost at once. They sit silent while she answers it.*

[47]

Miss Hodge (*at telephone*): 'Allo! 'Allo—yes——
She holds out the telephone to Leo.
'Ere, it's for you.

Leo (*hopelessly*): Dear God!
He takes it and Miss Hodge *goes out*.
Hallo!—Yes, speaking.—*Evening Standard?*—Oh, all right, send him up.

Gilda: This is a horrible morning.

Leo: I'm sorry.

Gilda: You needn't be.   It isn't your fault.

Leo: Yes, it is, I'm afraid.   I happen to have written a successful play.

Gilda (*exasperated*): Oh, really——
She turns away.

Leo: Well, it's true, isn't it?   That's what's upsetting you?

Gilda: Do you honestly think that?

Leo: I don't know.   I don't know what to think. This looks like a row but it hasn't even the virtue of being a new row.   We've had it before several times, and just lately more than ever.   It's inevitable that the more successful I become, the more people will run after me. I don't believe in their friendship, and I don't take them seriously, but I enjoy them.   Probably a damn sight more than they enjoy me!   I enjoy the whole thing. I've worked hard for it all my life.   Let them all come! They'll drop me, all right, when they're tired of me; but maybe I shall get tired first.

Gilda: I hope you will.

Leo: What does it matter, anyhow?

Gilda: It matters a lot.

Leo: I don't see why.

[*48*]

GILDA: They waste your time, these ridiculous celebrity hunters, and they sap your vitality.

LEO: Let them! I've got lots of time and lots of vitality.

GILDA: That's bravado. You're far too much of an artist to mean that, really.

LEO: I'm far too much of an artist to be taken in by the old cliché of shutting out the world and living for my art alone. There's just as much bunk in that as there is in a cocktail party at the Ritz.

GILDA: Something's gone. Don't you see?

LEO: Of course something's gone. Something always goes. The whole business of living is a process of readjustments. What are you mourning for? The dear old careless days of the Quartier Latin, when Laife was Laife!

GILDA: Don't be such a fool!

LEO: Let's dress up poor, and go back and pretend, shall we?

GILDA: Why not? That, at least, would be a definite disillusionment.

LEO: Certainly, it would. Standing over the skeletons of our past delights and trying to kick them to life again. That wouldn't be wasting time, would it?

GILDA: We needn't go back, or dress up poor, in order to pretend. We can pretend here. Among all this—— (*She kicks the newspapers.*) With the trumpets blowing and the flags flying and the telephone ringing, we can still pretend. We can pretend that we're happy.

> *She goes out of the room as the telephone rings.* LEO *stands looking after her for a moment, and then goes to the desk.*

[*49*]

LEO (*at telephone*): Hallo!—What?—Yes, speaking.—
Very well, I'll hold the line——

    MISS HODGE *comes in from the hall.*

MISS HODGE: There's a gentleman to see you. He
says he's from the *Evening Standard.*

LEO: Show him in.

    MISS HODGE *goes out.*

LEO (*at telephone*): Hallo—yes! Hallo there, how are
you? Of course, for hours, reading the papers.—Yes, all
of them marvellous——

    MR. BIRBECK *enters.* LEO *motions him to sit down.*
I'm so glad—it was thrilling, wasn't it?—Did he really?
That's grand!—Nonsense, it's always nice to hear things
like that—of course, I'd love to.—Black tie or white tie—
no tie at all! That'll be much more comfortable.—
Good-bye.—What?—No, really? So soon? You'll know
it by heart.—Yes, rather.—Good-bye!

    He hangs up the telephone.
I'm so sorry.

MR. BIRBECK (*shaking hands*): I'm from the *Standard.*

LEO: Yes, I know.

MR. BIRBECK: I've brought a photographer. I hope
you don't mind? We thought a little study of you in
your own home would be novel and interesting.

LEO (*bitterly*): I'm sure it would.

MR. BIRBECK: First of all, may I ask you a few questions?

LEO: Certainly, go ahead. Cigarette?

MR. BIRBECK: No, thank you. I'm not a smoker myself.

LEO (*taking one and lighting it*): I am.

MR. BIRBECK (*producing notebook*): This is not your
first play, is it?

Leo: No, my seventh.   Two of them have been produced in London within the last three years.

Mr. Birbeck: What were their names?

Leo: *The Swift River* and *Mrs. Draper.*

Mr. Birbeck: How do you spell "Mrs. Draper"?

Leo: The usual way—m r s   d r a p e r.

Mr. Birbeck: Do you care for sport?

Leo: Yes, madly.

Mr. Birbeck: Which particular sport do you like best?

Leo: No particular one.   I'm crazy about them all.

Mr. Birbeck: I see.

   He writes.

Do you believe the talkies will kill the theatre?

Leo: No.   I think they'll kill the talkies.

Mr. Birbeck (*laughing*): That's very good, that is! It really is.

Leo: Not as good as all that.

Mr. Birbeck: There's a question that interests our lady readers very much——

Leo: What's that?

Mr. Birbeck: What is your opinion of the modern girl?

Leo (*without flinching*): Downright; straightforward; upright.

Mr. Birbeck: You approve of the modern girl, then?

Leo: I didn't say so.

Mr. Birbeck: What are your ideas on marriage?

Leo: Garbled.

Mr. Birbeck: That's good, that is.   Very good!

Leo (*rising*): Don't put it, though—don't write down any of this interview; come and see me again.

MR. BIRBECK: Why, what's wrong?

LEO: The whole thing's wrong, Mr.——

MR. BIRBECK: Birbeck.

LEO: Mr. Birbeck.   The whole business is grotesque. Don't you see how grotesque it is?

MR. BIRBECK: I'm afraid I don't understand.

LEO: Don't you ever feel sick inside when you have to ask those questions?

MR. BIRBECK: No, why should I?

LEO: Will you do me a very great favour?

MR. BIRBECK: What is it?

LEO: Call in your photographer.   Photograph me— and leave me alone.

MR. BIRBECK (*offended*): Certainly.

LEO: Don't think me rude.   I'm just rather tired, that's all.

MR. BIRBECK: I quite understand.

He goes out into the hall and returns in a moment with the photographer.

Where do you think would be best?

LEO: Wherever you say.

MR. BIRBECK: Just here?

LEO (*taking his stand just in front of the desk*): All right.

MR. BIRBECK: Perhaps I could come and see you again sometime when you're not so tired?

LEO: Yes, of course.   Telephone me.

MR. BIRBECK: Tomorrow?

LEO: Yes, tomorrow.

MR. BIRBECK: About eleven?

LEO: Yes.   About eleven.

MR. BIRBECK: Now, then—are you ready?

GILDA *comes out of the bedroom, dressed for the street. She goes over to* LEO *and puts her arms round his neck.*

GILDA: I'm going to do a little shopping—— (*Then softly*): Sorry, darling——

LEO: All right, sweet.

GILDA *goes out.*

MR. BIRBECK: Just a little smile!

LEO *smiles as the curtain falls.*

END OF ACT TWO: SCENE I

ACT TWO

SCENE II

ACT TWO: Scene II

THE SCENE *is the same, a few days later.*

It is evening, and MISS HODGE *has just finished laying a cold supper on a bridge table in front of the sofa. She regards it thoughtfully for a moment, and then goes to the bedroom door.*

MISS HODGE: Your supper's all ready, ma'am.

GILDA (*in bedroom*): Thank you, Miss Hodge. I shan't want you any more tonight, then.

MISS HODGE *goes off into the kitchen.* GILDA *comes out of the bedroom. She is wearing pyjamas and a dressing gown. She goes over to the desk, on which there is a parcel of books. She undoes the parcel and scrutinizes the books, humming happily to herself as she does so.* MISS HODGE *reënters from the kitchen, this time in her coat and hat.*

GILDA: Hello, Miss Hodge! I thought you'd gone.

MISS HODGE: I was just putting on me 'at. I think you'll find everything you want there.

GILDA: I'm sure I shall. Thank you.

MISS HODGE: Not at all; it's a pleasure, I'm sure.

GILDA: Oh, Miss Hodge, do you think it would be a good idea if Mr. Mercuré and I got married?

MISS HODGE: I thought you was married.

GILDA: Oh, I'd forgotten. We never told you, did we?

[*57*]

MISS HODGE: You certainly didn't.

GILDA: Well, we're not.

MISS HODGE (*thoughtfully*): Oh, I see.

GILDA: Are you shocked?

MISS HODGE: It's no affair of mine, ma'am—miss.

GILDA: What do you think about marriage?

MISS HODGE: Not very much, miss, having had a basinful meself, in a manner of speaking.

GILDA (*surprised*): What!

MISS HODGE: Hodge is my maiden name. I took it back in—in disgust, if you know what I mean.

GILDA: Have you been married much, then?

MISS HODGE: Twice, all told.

GILDA: Where are your husbands now?

MISS HODGE: One's dead, and the other's in Newcastle.

GILDA (*smiling*): Oh.

MISS HODGE: Well, I'll be getting 'ome now, if there's nothing else you require?

GILDA: No, there's nothing else, thank you. Goodnight.

MISS HODGE: Good-night, miss.

> MISS HODGE *goes out.* GILDA *laughs to herself; pours herself out a glass of Sherry from the bottle on the table, and settles onto the sofa with the books.* OTTO *comes in from the hall and stands in the doorway, looking at her.*

OTTO: Hallo, Gilda!

GILDA (*turning sharply and staring at him*): It's not true!

OTTO (*coming into the room*): Here we are again!

GILDA: Oh, Otto!

OTTO: Are you pleased?

GILDA: I don't quite know yet.

OTTO: Make up your mind, there's a dear.

GILDA: I'll try.

OTTO: Where's Leo?

GILDA: Away. He went away this afternoon.

OTTO: This seems a very nice flat.

GILDA: It is. You can see right across to the other side of the square on a clear day.

OTTO: I've only just arrived.

GILDA: Where from?

OTTO: New York. I had an exhibition there.

GILDA: Was it successful?

OTTO: Very, thank you.

GILDA: I've decided quite definitely now: I'm ecstatically pleased to see you.

OTTO: That's lovely.

GILDA: How did you get in?

OTTO: I met an odd-looking woman going out. She opened the door for me.

GILDA: That was Miss Hodge. She's had two husbands.

OTTO: I once met a woman who'd had four husbands.

GILDA: Aren't you going to take off your hat and coat?

OTTO: Don't you like them?

GILDA: Enormously. It was foolish of me to ask whether your exhibition was successful. I can see it was! Your whole personality reeks of it.

OTTO (*taking off his hat and coat*): I'm disappointed that Leo isn't here.

GILDA: He'll be back on Monday.

OTTO: How is he, please?

GILDA: Awfully well.

OTTO: Oh, dear! Oh, dear, oh, dear—I feel very funny! I feel as if I were going to cry, and I don't want to cry a bit.

GILDA: Let's both cry, just a little!

OTTO: Darling, darling Gilda!

They rush into each other's arms and hug each other.

OTTO: It's all, all right now, isn't it?

GILDA: More than all right.

OTTO: I was silly to stay away so long, wasn't I?

GILDA: That was what Leo meant the other morning when he said he knew what was missing.

OTTO: Me?

GILDA: Of course.

OTTO: I'm terribly glad he said that.

GILDA: We were having a row, trying to find out why we weren't quite as happy as we should be.

OTTO: Do you have many rows?

GILDA: Quite a lot, every now and then.

OTTO: As many as we used to?

GILDA: About the same. There's a bit of trouble on at the moment, really. He's getting too successful and sought after. I'm worried about him.

OTTO: You needn't be. It won't touch him—inside.

GILDA: I'm afraid, all the same; they're all so shrill and foolish, clacking at him.

OTTO: I read about the play in the train. It's a riot, isn't it?

GILDA: Capacity—every performance.

OTTO: Is it good?

GILDA: Yes, I think so.

OTTO: Only think so?

GILDA: Three scenes are first rate, especially the last act. The beginning of the second act drags a bit, and most of the first act's too facile—you know what I mean —he flips along with easy swift dialogue, but doesn't go deep enough. It's all very well played.

OTTO: We'll go on Monday night.

GILDA: Will you stay, now that you've come back?

OTTO: I expect so. It depends on Leo.

GILDA: Oh!

OTTO: He may not want me to.

GILDA: I think he'll want you to, even more than I do!

OTTO: Why do you say that?

GILDA: I don't know. It came up suddenly, like a hiccup.

OTTO: I feel perfectly cozy about the whole business now, you know—no trailing ends of resentment—I'm clear and clean, a newly washed lamb, bleating for company!

GILDA: Would you like some Sherry?

OTTO: Very much indeed.

GILDA: Here, have my glass. I'll get another. We'll need another plate as well and a knife and fork.

OTTO (*looking over the table*): Cold ham, salad; what's that blob in the pie dish?

GILDA: Cold rice pudding. Delicious! You can have jam with it and cream.

OTTO (*without enthusiasm*): How glorious.

> GILDA *runs into the kitchen and returns in a moment with plate and knife and fork, etc.*

GILDA: Here we are!

OTTO: I expected more grandeur.

GILDA: Butlers and footmen?

[*61*]

OTTO: Yes, just a few. Concealed lighting, too. There's something a thought sordid about that lamp over there. Did you decorate this room?

GILDA: You know perfectly well I didn't.

OTTO: Well, you should.

GILDA: Do you want anything stronger to drink than Sherry?

OTTO: No, Sherry's all right. It's gentle and refined, and imparts a discreet glow. Of course, I'm used to having biscuits with it.

GILDA: There aren't any biscuits.

OTTO (*magnificently*): It doesn't matter.

GILDA: Do sit down, darling.

OTTO (*drawing up a chair*): What delicious-looking ham! Where *did* you get it?

GILDA: I have it specially sent from Scotland.

OTTO: Why Scotland?

GILDA: It lives there when it's alive.

OTTO: A bonny country, Scotland, if all I've heard is correct, what with the banshees wailing and the four-leaved shamrock.

GILDA: That's Ireland, dear.

OTTO: Never mind. The same wistful dampness distinguishes them both.

GILDA (*helping him to ham*): I knew you'd arrive soon.

OTTO (*helping her to salad*): Where's Leo gone, exactly?

GILDA: Smart house party in Hampshire. Bridge, backgammon, several novelists, and a squash court that nobody uses.

OTTO: The Decoration of Life—that's what that is.

GILDA: Slightly out of drawing, but terribly amusing.

[*62*]

Otto: It won't last long.   Don't worry.

Gilda: Tell me where you've been, please, and what you've seen and what you've done.   Is your painting still good, or has it deteriorated just a little?   I'm suspicious, you see!   Dreadfully suspicious of people liking things too much—things that matter, I mean.   There's too much enthusiasm for Art going on nowadays.   It smears out the highlights.

Otto: You're certainly in a state, aren't you?

Gilda: Yes, I am.   And it's getting worse.

Otto: Turbulent!   Downright turbulent.

Gilda: There isn't any mustard.

Otto: Never mind: I don't want any, do you?

Gilda: I don't know, really.   I'm always a little undecided about mustard.

Otto: It might pep up the rice pudding!

Gilda: Strange, isn't it?   This going on where we left off?

Otto: Not quite where we left off, thank God.

Gilda: Wasn't it horrible?

Otto: I was tortured with regrets for a long while.   I felt I ought to have knocked Leo down.

Gilda: I'm awfully glad you didn't.   He hates being knocked down.

Otto: Then, of course, he might have retaliated and knocked me down!

Gilda: You're bigger than he is.

Otto: He's more wiry.   He once held me in the bath for twenty minutes while he poured cold water over me.

Gilda (*laughing*): Yes, I know!

Otto (*laughing too*): Oh, of course—that's what you were both laughing at when I came in that day, wasn't it?

[*63*]

GILDA (*weakly*): Yes, it was very, very unfortunate.

OTTO: An unkind trick of Fate's, to have dropped it into your minds just then.

GILDA: It made a picture, you see—an unbearably comic picture—we were both terribly strained and unhappy; our nerves were stretched like elastic, and that snapped it.

OTTO: I think that upset me more than anything.

GILDA: You might have known it wasn't you we were laughing at.   Not you, yourself.

OTTO: It's exactly a hundred and twenty-seven years ago today.

GILDA: A hundred and twenty-eight.

OTTO: We've grown up since then.

GILDA: I do hope so, just a little.

OTTO: I went away on a freight boat, you know.   I went for thousands of miles and I was very unhappy indeed.

GILDA: And very seasick, I should think.

OTTO: Only the first few days.

GILDA: Not steadily?

OTTO: As steadily as one can be seasick.

GILDA: Do you know a lot about ships now?

OTTO: Not a thing.   The whole business still puzzles me dreadfully.   I know about starboard and port, of course, and all the different bells; but no one has yet been able to explain to me satisfactorily why, the first moment a rough sea occurs, the whole thing doesn't turn upside down!

GILDA: Were you frightened?

OTTO: Petrified, but I got used to it.

GILDA: Was it an English ship?

OTTO: No, Norwegian.   I can say, "How do you do?" in Norwegian.

GILDA: We must get to know some Norwegian people immediately, so that you can say "How do you do?" to them.—Where are your pictures?

OTTO: Not unpacked yet.   They're at the Carlton.

GILDA: The Carlton!   You haven't gone "grand" on me, too, have you?

OTTO: I have, indeed.   I've got several commissions to do portraits here in London.   The very best people. I only paint the very best people.

GILDA (*almost snappily*): They have such interesting faces, haven't they?

OTTO (*reproachfully*): I don't paint their faces, Gilda. Fourth dimensional, that's what I am.   I paint their souls.

GILDA: You'd have to be eighth dimensional and clairvoyant to find them.

OTTO: I'm grieved to see that Leo has done little or nothing towards taming your proud revolutionary spirit.

GILDA: He's inflamed it.

OTTO: I know what's wrong with you, my sweet. You're just the concentrated essence of "Love Among the Artists."

GILDA: I think that was unkind.

OTTO: If you were creative yourself you'd understand better.   As it is, you know a lot.   You know an awful lot. Your critical faculty is first rate.   I'd rather have your opinion on paintings or books or plays than anyone else's I know.   But you're liable to get sidetracked if you're not careful.   Life is for living first and foremost.   Even for artists, life is for living.   Remember that.

[*65*]

GILDA: You have grown up, haven't you?

OTTO: In the beginning, when we were all in Paris, everything was really very much easier to manage, even our emotional problems. Leo and I were both struggling, a single line was in both our minds leading to success— that's what we were planning for, working like dogs for! You helped us both, jostling us onto the line again when we slipped off, and warming us when we were cold in discouragement. You picked on me to love a little bit more, because you decided, rightly then, that I was the weaker. They were very happy, those days, and glamour will always cling to them in our memories. But don't be misled by them; don't make the mistake of trying to recapture the spirit of them. That's dead, along with our early loves and dreams and quarrels, and all the rest of the foolishness.

GILDA: I think I want to cry again.

OTTO: There's nothing like a good cry.

GILDA: You can't blame me for hating success, when it changes all the—the things I love best.

OTTO: Things would have changed, anyhow. It isn't only success that does it—it's time and experience and new circumstances.

GILDA (*bitterly*): Was it the Norwegians that taught you this still wisdom? They must be wonderful people.

OTTO (*gently*): No, I was alone. I just sat quietly and looked at everything.

GILDA: I see.

OTTO: Would you fancy a little more salad?

GILDA: No, thank you.

OTTO: Then it's high time we started on the cold rice pudding.

[*66*]

GILDA: I see one thing clearly.

OTTO (*smiling*): What?

GILDA: I'm not needed any more.

OTTO: I thought you were going to say that.

GILDA: It's what you meant me to say, isn't it?

OTTO: We shall always need each other, all three of us.

GILDA: Nonsense! The survival of the fittest—that's what counts.

OTTO: Do have some rice pudding?

GILDA: To hell with you and the rice pudding!

OTTO (*helping himself*): Hard words. Hard, cruel words!

GILDA: You're so sure of yourself, aren't you? You're both so sure of yourselves, you and Leo. Getting what you want must be terribly gratifying!

OTTO (*unruffled*): It is.

GILDA (*suddenly smiling*): Do you remember how I used to rail and roar against being feminine?

OTTO: Yes, dear. You were very noisy about the whole business.

GILDA: I'm suddenly glad about it for the first time. Do you want some jam with that?

OTTO: What sort of jam is it?

GILDA: Strawberry, I think.

OTTO: Of course, I'm used to having dark plum with rice pudding, but I'll make do with strawberry.

GILDA: I'll get it!

She goes into the kitchen. The telephone rings. OTTO answers it.

OTTO (*at telephone*): Hallo!—Hallo—yes, speaking.— Didn't you recognize my voice?—How absurd! It must be a bad line.—Dinner on the seventh? Yes, I should

[*67*]

love to.—You don't mind if I come as Marie Antoinette, do you? I have to go to a fancy dress ball.—Where? Oh, my aunt is giving it—yes, in a bad house, she runs a whole chain of them, you know!—Thank you so much.

He hangs up the telephone.

GILDA (*reëntering*): I put it into a glass dish. Who was that?

OTTO: Somebody called Brevell, Lady Brevell. She wants Leo to dine on the seventh. I accepted.

GILDA: Good! You can both go. I'm sure she'd be delighted.

OTTO (*sitting down again*): What! No cream?

GILDA: It was a delusion about the cream. I thought there was a lot, but there isn't a drop.

OTTO: I think you've improved in looks really with the passing of the years.

GILDA: How sweet, Otto! I'm so pleased.

OTTO: Your skin, for instance. Your skin's much better.

GILDA: It ought to be, I've been taking a lot of trouble with it.

OTTO: What sort of trouble?

GILDA: Oh, just having it pushed and rubbed and slapped about.

OTTO: Funny, how much in love with you I was!

GILDA: We'll have a good laugh about it when you've finished your pudding.

OTTO: What's happened to Ernest?

GILDA: He's been away, too, a long way away; he went on a world cruise with a lot of old ladies in straw hats!

[*68*]

OTTO: Dear little Ernest!

GILDA: I saw him a few weeks ago, then he went back to Paris.

OTTO: An odd life.   Sterile, don't you think?

GILDA: You've certainly emancipated yourself into a grand complacency.

OTTO: If you're unkind to me, I shall go back to the Carlton.

GILDA: Have you got a suite, or just a common bedroom and bath?

OTTO: Darling, I do love you so very much!

GILDA: A nice comfortable love, without heart throbs.

OTTO: Are you trying to lure me to your wanton bed?

GILDA: What would you do if I did?

OTTO: Probably enjoy it very much.

GILDA: I doubt if I should.

OTTO: Have I changed so dreadfully?

GILDA (*maliciously*): It isn't you that's changed—it's time and experience and new circumstances!

OTTO (*rising*): I've finished my supper.   It wasn't very good but it sufficed.   I should now like a whiskey and soda.

GILDA: It's in that thing over there.

OTTO (*getting it out*): It is a thing, isn't it?   Do you want one?

GILDA: No, I don't think so.

OTTO: Just a little one?

GILDA: All right.

OTTO (*pouring them out*): If we were bored, we could always go to the pictures, couldn't we?

GILDA: It's too late; we shouldn't get in to anything that's worth seeing.

[*69*]

Otto: Oh, how disappointing! How very, very, very disappointing!

Gilda: Personally, I'm enjoying myself here.

Otto (*handing her her drink*): Are you, indeed?

Gilda: Yes. This measured skirmishing is delightful.

Otto: Be careful, won't you? I do implore you to be careful!

Gilda: I never was. Why should I start now?

Otto (*raising his glass*): I salute your spirit of defiance, my dearest.

Gilda (*raising her glass*): Yours, too.

Otto (*shaking his head*): A bad business; a very bad business.

Gilda: Love among the artists.

Otto: Love among anybody.

Gilda: Perhaps not love, exactly. Something a little below it and a little above it, but something terribly strong.

Otto: Meaning this?

Gilda: Of course. What else?

Otto: We should have principles to hang on to, you know. This floating about without principles is so very dangerous.

Gilda: Life is for living.

Otto: You accused me of being too sure. It's you who are sure now.

Gilda: Sure of what?

Otto: Sure that I want you.

Gilda: Don't you?

Otto: Of course I do.

Gilda: Keep away, then, a minute, and let me look at you all over again.

Otto: I used to sit on the top deck of that freighter, and shut my eyes and see you standing there, just like you are now.

Gilda: Good old romance, bobbing up again and wrapping up our crudities in a few veils!

Otto: Shut up! Don't talk like that.

Gilda: I'm not nearly as afraid as you are.

Otto: You haven't got so much to lose.

Gilda: How do you know? You've forgotten everything about me—the real me. That dim figure you conjured up under your damned tropic stars was an illusion, a misty ghost, scratched out of a few memories, inaccurate, untrue—nothing to do with me in any way. This is me, now! Take a good look and see if you can tell what I have to lose in the game, or to win, either—perhaps you can tell that, too! Can you? Can you?

Otto: You look so terribly sweet when you're angry.

Gilda: Another illusion. I'm not sweet.

Otto: Those were only love words. You mustn't be so crushing. How are we to conduct this revivalist meeting without love words?

Gilda: Let's keep them under control.

Otto: I warn you it's going to be very difficult. You've worked yourself up into a frenzy of sophistication. You've decided on being calculating and disillusioned and brazen, even slightly coarse over the affair. That's all very well, but how long is it going to last? That's what I ask myself. How long is it going to last—this old wanton mood of yours?

Gilda (*breaking down*): Don't—don't laugh at me.

Otto: I must—a little.

[*71*]

GILDA: It's an unfair advantage. You've both got it, and you both use it against me mercilessly.

OTTO: Laugh, too; it's not so serious, really.

GILDA: If I once started, I should never stop. That's a warning.

OTTO: Duly registered.

GILDA: What are we going to do about Leo?

OTTO: Wait and see what he's going to do about us.

GILDA: Haven't you got any shame at all?

OTTO: Just about as much as you have.

GILDA: The whole thing's degrading, completely and utterly degrading.

OTTO: Only when measured up against other people's standards.

GILDA: Why should we flatter ourselves that we're so tremendously different?

OTTO: Flattery doesn't enter into it. We are different. Our lives are diametrically opposed to ordinary social conventions; and it's no use grabbing at those conventions to hold us up when we find we're in deep water. We've jilted them and eliminated them, and we've got to find our own solutions for our own peculiar moral problems.

GILDA: Very glib, very glib indeed, and very plausible.

OTTO: It's true. There's no sense in stamping about and saying how degrading it all is. Of course it's degrading; according to a certain code, the whole situation's degrading and always has been. The Methodists wouldn't approve of us, and the Catholics wouldn't either; and the Evangelists and the Episcopalians and the Anglicans and the Christian Scientists—I don't suppose even the Polynesian Islanders would think very highly of us, but they wouldn't mind quite so much, being so far away. They could all club together—the whole lot of them—and say with perfect truth, according to their lights, that we were loose-living, irreligious, unmoral degenerates, couldn't they?

GILDA (*meekly*): Yes, Otto, I expect so.

OTTO: But the whole point is, it's none of their business. We're not doing any harm to anyone else. We're not peppering the world with illegitimate children. The only people we could possibly mess up are ourselves, and that's our lookout. It's no use you trying to decide which you love best, Leo or me, because you don't know! At the moment, it's me, because you've been living with Leo for a long time and I've been away. A gay, ironic chance threw the three of us together and tied our lives into a tight knot at the outset. To deny it would be ridiculous, and to unravel it impossible. Therefore, the only thing left is to enjoy it thoroughly, every rich moment of it, every thrilling second——

GILDA: Come off your soap box, and stop ranting!

OTTO: I want to make love to you very badly indeed, please! I've been lonely for a long time without you; now I've come back, and I'm not going to be lonely any more. Believe me, loneliness is a mug's game.

GILDA: The whole thing's a mug's game.

OTTO: You're infinitely lovely to me, darling, and so very necessary. The circle has swung round, and it's my turn again—that's only fair, isn't it?

GILDA: I—I suppose so.

OTTO: If you didn't want me, it would be different, but you do—you do, my dearest dear!—I can see it in your eyes. You want me every bit as much as I want you!

GILDA (*with a little smile*): Yes, every bit.

OTTO: This is a moment to remember, all right. Scribble it onto your heart; a flicker of ecstasy sandwiched between yesterday and tomorrow—something to be recaptured in the future without illusion, perfect in itself! Don't let's forget this—whatever else happens, don't let's forget this.

GILDA: How easy it all seems in this light.

OTTO: What small perverse meanness in you forbids you to walk round the sofa to me?

GILDA: I couldn't move, if the house was on fire!

OTTO: I believe it is.   To hell with the sofa!

> *He vaults over it and takes her in his arms. They stand holding each other closely and gradually subside onto the sofa.*

OTTO (*kissing her*): Hvordan staar det til!

GILDA (*blissfully*): What's that, darling?

OTTO: "How do you do?" in Norwegian.

The curtain slowly falls.

END OF ACT TWO: SCENE 2

ACT TWO

Scene III

ACT TWO: Scene III

THE SCENE *is the same. It is about ten-thirty the next morning.*

As the curtain rises, MISS HODGE *shows* ERNEST FRIEDMAN *into the room.*

MISS HODGE: I will tell madam—miss—madam you're here, sir.

ERNEST: Why so much confusion, Miss Hodge?

MISS HODGE: I was only told last night, sir, that—er, well—that—er——

ERNEST: Oh, I see.

MISS HODGE: It's a bit muddling at first, in a manner of speaking, but I shall get used to it.

ERNEST: I'm sure you will.

MISS HODGE goes into the bedroom, and returns again in a moment with very pursed-up lips.

MISS HODGE (*coldly*): She will be in in a moment, sir.

MISS HODGE goes into the kitchen and slams the door. ERNEST *looks after her in some astonishment.*

GILDA *enters. She is fully dressed, wearing a hat and coat.*

GILDA (*with tremendous gaiety*): Ernest! What a surprise!

ERNEST: What's the matter with Miss Hodge?

GILDA: The matter with her? I don't know—I haven't examined her.

[77]

ERNEST: It was foolish of you to tell her you and Leo weren't married.

GILDA: It slipped out; I'd forgotten she didn't know. Have you come from Paris?

ERNEST: Yes, last night.   There's been a slight argument going on for weeks.

GILDA: Argument?   What kind of an argument?

ERNEST: One of those Holbein arguments.

GILDA: Somebody said it wasn't, I suppose?

ERNEST: Yes, that's it.

GILDA: Was it?

ERNEST: In my humble opinion, yes.

GILDA: Did your humble opinion settle it?

ERNEST: I hope so.

GILDA: Admirable.   Quiet, sure, perfect conviction—absolutely admirable.

ERNEST: Thank you, Gilda.   Don't imagine that the irony in your tone escaped me.

GILDA: That wasn't irony; it was envy.

ERNEST: It's high time you stopped envying me.

GILDA: I don't think I ever shall.

ERNEST: How's Leo?

GILDA: Not very well.

ERNEST: What's wrong with him?

GILDA: Tummy; he's had an awful night.   He didn't close an eye until about five, but he's fast asleep now.

ERNEST: I'm sorry. I wanted to say good-bye to you both.

GILDA: Good-bye?

ERNEST: I'm going back to Paris this afternoon and sailing for America on Wednesday.

GILDA: You do flip about, don't you, Ernest?

ERNEST: Not any more. I've decided to live in New York permanently. I've been angling for a particular penthouse for years and now I've got it.

GILDA: How lovely. Is it very high?

ERNEST: About thirty floors.

GILDA (*gaily*): Do you want a housekeeper?

ERNEST: Yes, badly. Will you come?

GILDA: Perhaps.

She laughs.

ERNEST: You seem very gay this morning.

GILDA: I'm always gay on Sundays. There's something intoxicating about Sunday in London.

ERNEST: It's excellent about the play. I read all the reviews.

GILDA: Yes, it's grand. It ought to run for years and years and years and years and years!

ERNEST: I suppose Leo's delighted.

GILDA: Absolutely hysterical. I think that's what's upset his stomach. He was always oversensitive, you know; even in Paris in the old days he used to roll about in agony at the least encouragement, don't you remember?

ERNEST: No, I can't say that I do.

GILDA: That's because you're getting a bit "gaga," darling! You've sold too many pictures and made too much money and travelled too much. That world cruise was a fatal mistake. I thought so at the time, but I didn't say anything about it, because I didn't want to upset you. But going round in a troupe, with all those tatty old girls, must have been very, very bad for you. I expected every day to get a wire from somewhere or other saying you'd died of something or other.

ERNEST: Do stop, you're making me giddy.

GILDA: Perhaps you'd like a little Sherry?

ERNEST: No, thank you.

GILDA: It's very good Sherry; dry as a bone!

ERNEST: You seem to me to be in a very strange mood, Gilda.

GILDA: I've never felt better in my life. Ups and downs! My life is one long convulsive sequence of Ups and Downs. This is an Up—at least, I think it is.

ERNEST: You're sure it's not nervous collapse?

GILDA: I never thought of that; it's a very good idea. I shall have a nervous collapse!

ERNEST: Will you ever change, I wonder? Will you ever change into a quieter, more rational person?

GILDA: Why should I?

ERNEST: What's wrong now?

GILDA: Wrong! What could be wrong? Everything's right. Righter than it's ever been before. God's in His heaven, all's right with the world—I always thought that was a remarkably silly statement, didn't you?

ERNEST: Unreasoning optimism is always slightly silly, but it's a great comfort to, at least, three quarters of the human race.

GILDA: The human race is a let-down, Ernest; a bad, bad let-down! I'm disgusted with it. It thinks it's progressed but it hasn't; it thinks it's risen above the primeval slime but it hasn't—it's still wallowing in it! It's still clinging to us, clinging to our hair and our eyes and our souls. We've invented a few small things that make noises, but we haven't invented one big thing that creates quiet, endless peaceful quiet—something to pull over us like a gigantic eiderdown; something to deaden the sound of our emotional yellings and screechings and suffocate our psychological confusions——

ERNEST (*weakly*): I think, perhaps, I would like a glass of Sherry after all.

GILDA (*going to the "thing"*): It's all right, Ernest, don't be frightened! You're always a safety valve for me. I think, during the last few years, I've screamed at you more than anyone else in the world.

She hands him the bottle.

Here you are.

ERNEST (*looking at it*): This is brandy.

GILDA: So it is. How stupid of me.

She finds the Sherry and two glasses.

Here we are!

ERNEST (*putting the brandy bottle on the desk*): I'm not sure that I find it very comfortable, being a safety valve!

GILDA: It's the penalty you pay for being sweet and sympathetic, and very old indeed.

ERNEST (*indignantly*): I'm not very old indeed!

GILDA: Only in wisdom and experience, darling.

She pours out Sherry for them both.

Here's to you, Ernest, and me, too!

They both drink.

ERNEST: Now, then?

GILDA: Now then, what?

ERNEST: Out with it!

GILDA: Take my advice, my dear; run like a stag—be fleet of foot! Beat it!

ERNEST: Why?

GILDA: I'm a lone woman. I'm unattached. I'm free.

ERNEST: Oh! Oh, are you, really!

GILDA: I'm cured. I'm not a prisoner any more.

[*81*]

I've let myself out.   This is a day of great exaltation for me.

ERNEST: I'm sure I'm delighted to hear it.

GILDA (*with the suspicion of a catch in her voice*): I'm not needed any more—I'm going.

ERNEST: Where are you going?

GILDA: I haven't the faintest idea.   The world is wide, far too wide and round, too.   I can scamper round and round it, like a white rat in a cage!

ERNEST: That will be very tiring.

GILDA: Not so tiring as staying still; at least, I might preserve the illusion that I'm getting somewhere.

ERNEST (*prosaically*): Have you had a row with Leo?

GILDA: No; I haven't had a row with anyone.   I've just seen the light suddenly.   I saw it last night.   The survival of the fittest, that's the light.   Didn't you know?

ERNEST: I think, perhaps, I should understand better if you spoke in Russian.

GILDA: Or Norwegian.   There's a fascinating language for you!

ERNEST: I believe there is a very nice nursing home in Manchester Street.

GILDA (*taking a note out of her bag*): You see this?

ERNEST: Yes.

GILDA: It's for Leo.

ERNEST: To read when he wakes up?

GILDA: Yes.   If he ever wakes up.

ERNEST: You haven't poisoned him, have you?

GILDA: No; but he's nearly poisoned me!   An insidious, dreary sort of poison, a lymphatic poison, turning me slowly into a cow.

ERNEST (*laughing*): My poor Gilda!

GILDA (*propping it up against the brandy bottle*): I shall leave it here.

ERNEST: Pity there isn't a pin cushion.

GILDA: I expect you think I'm being overdramatic?

ERNEST: Not any more than usual.

GILDA: Well, I'm not. I'm perfectly calm inside. Cold as steel.

ERNEST: Can one be exalted and cold as steel at the same time?

GILDA: I can. I can be lots of things at the same time; it becomes a great bore after a while. In the future, I intend to be only òne thing.

ERNEST: That being——?

GILDA: Myself, Ernest. My unadulterated self! Myself, without hangings, without trimmings, unencumbered by the winding tendrils of other people's demands——

ERNEST: That was very nicely put.

GILDA: You can laugh at me as much as you like. I give everybody free permission to laugh at me. I can laugh at myself, too, now—for the first time, and enjoy it.

ERNEST: Can you?

GILDA: Yes; isn't it lovely?

ERNEST: I congratulate you.

GILDA: I'm glad you suddenly appeared this morning to say good-bye—very appropriate! It's a day of good-byes—the air's thick with them. You have a tremendous sense of the "right moment," Ernest. It's wonderful. You pop up like a genie out of a bottle, just to be in at the death! You really ought to have been a priest.

ERNEST: Are you really serious? Are you really going?

GILDA: I've never been more serious in my life. Of course I'm going—I've got to learn a few things while there's still time—who knows, I might even learn to be an artist! Just think of that! And even if I can't quite achieve such—such splendour, there are other lessons for me. There's the lesson of paddling my own canoe, for instance—not just weighing down somebody else's and imagining I'm steering it!

ERNEST: Oh, I see. I see it all now.

GILDA: No, you don't—not all; just a little, perhaps, but not all.

ERNEST: Where are you going, really?

GILDA: First, to a hotel, to make a few plans.

ERNEST: You can take over my room at the Carlton, if you like. I'm leaving today.

GILDA (*laughing hysterically*): The Carlton! Oh, no, Ernest, not the Carlton!

ERNEST: Why, what's the matter with it?

GILDA: It's too big and pink and grand for me. I want a decayed hotel; gentle and sad and a little bit under the weather.

ERNEST: And afterwards?

GILDA: Paris—no, not Paris—Berlin. I'm very attached to Berlin.

ERNEST: Are you sure you're wise? This is rather—well, rather drastic, isn't it?

GILDA (*quietly*): I'm quite sure.

ERNEST: I won't try to dissuade you, then.

GILDA: No, don't. It wouldn't do any good. I'm quite determined.

ERNEST: I have an instinctive distrust of sudden impulses.

[*84*]

GILDA: I'll fool you yet! I'll make you eat your damned skepticism!

ERNEST (*smiling*): Sorry!

GILDA: Good-bye, Ernest. I'm going now.

ERNEST: You'll be very lonely. Aren't you afraid?

GILDA: I can bear it. I've been lonely before.

ERNEST: Not for a long while.

GILDA: Recently, quite—quite recently. Loneliness doesn't necessarily mean being by yourself.

ERNEST (*gently*): Very well, dear.

GILDA (*suddenly flinging her arms round his neck*): You're very tender and very kind and I'm tremendously grateful to you! Come on, let's go.

ERNEST: Haven't you got any bags or anything?

GILDA: I've packed a dressing case with all my immediate wants; I shall get everything else new, brand new——

> *She goes quietly to the bedroom door and gets a dressing case, which she has left just behind it.*

I'll drop you off at the Carlton, and take your taxi on.

ERNEST: Is he asleep?

GILDA: Fast asleep. Come on!

> *They go out into the hall. Suddenly* GILDA *is heard to say, "Just a moment, I've forgotten something!"*
>
> *She comes quickly back into the room, takes another letter out of her bag and props it up on the desk. Then she goes out.*
>
> *The front door is heard to slam very loudly.*
>
> *After a moment or two the telephone rings; it goes on ringing until* MISS HODGE *comes out of the kitchen and answers it.*

Miss Hodge (*at telephone*): 'Allo, 'allo!—What?—No, 'e's not—'e's away.—All right!—Not at all.

> *She slams down the telephone and goes back into the kitchen. Otto comes out of the bedroom. He is wearing a dressing gown and pyjamas belonging to Leo, and looks very sleepy. He finds a cigarette and lights it; then goes to the kitchen door.*

Otto (*calling*): Gilda!—Gilda, where are you?

> *Miss Hodge appears. Her face grim with disapproval.*

Miss Hodge: She's gone h'out.

Otto (*startled*): Oh! Did she say where?

Miss Hodge: She did not.

Otto: What's the time?

Miss Hodge: H'eleven.

Otto (*pleasantly*): We met last night on the door-step; do you remember?

Miss Hodge: Yes, I remember all right.

Otto: It was very kind of you to let me in.

Miss Hodge: I didn't know you was going to stay all night.

Otto: I wasn't sure, myself.

Miss Hodge: A pretty thing!

Otto: I beg your pardon?

Miss Hodge: I said, "A pretty thing" and I meant "A pretty thing"—nice goings on!

Otto (*amiably*): Very nice, thank you.

Miss Hodge: I'm a respectable woman.

Otto: Never mind.

Miss Hodge: I don't mind a little fun every now and then among friends, but I do draw the line at looseness!

Otto: You're making a mistake, Miss—Miss——?

[*86*]

MISS HODGE: Me name's 'Odge.

OTTO: You're making a mistake, Miss Odge.

MISS HODGE: 'Ow do you mean?

OTTO: You are making a mistake in daring to disapprove of something that has nothing to do with you whatever.

MISS HODGE (*astounded*): Well, I never!

OTTO: Please go away, and mind your own business.

MISS HODGE, *with a gasp of fury, flounces off into the kitchen.* OTTO *comes down to the sofa and lies on it with his back towards the door, blowing smoke rings into the air.*

The door opens and LEO *creeps into the room. He can only see the cigarette smoke,* OTTO'S *head being hidden by the cushion.*

LEO: Hallo, darling! I couldn't bear it any more, so I've come back.

OTTO (*sitting up slowly*): Hello, Leo.

LEO: You!

OTTO: Yes. I couldn't bear it any longer, either, so I've come back.

LEO: Where have you come from?

OTTO: New York.

LEO: When—when did you arrive?

OTTO: Last night.

LEO: Why—why aren't you dressed?

OTTO: I've only just got up.

LEO: You stayed here?

OTTO: Yes.

LEO (*slowly*): With Gilda?

OTTO: Yes.

LEO: I see.

[*87*]

OTTO: It wouldn't be any use lying, would it?   Pretending I didn't?

LEO: No use at all.

OTTO: I'm not even sorry, Leo, except for hurting you.

LEO: Where is Gilda?

OTTO: She's gone out.

LEO: Out!   Why?   Where's she gone to?

OTTO: I don't know.

LEO (*turning away*): How vile of you! How unspeakably vile of you both!

OTTO: It was inevitable.

LEO (*contemptuously*): Inevitable!

OTTO: I arrived unexpectedly; you were away; Gilda was alone.   I love her; I've always loved her—I've never stopped for a minute, and she loves me, too.

LEO: What about me?

OTTO: I told you I was sorry about hurting you.

LEO: Gilda loves me.

OTTO: I never said she didn't.

LEO (*hopelessly*): What are we to do?   What are we to do now?

OTTO: Do you know, I really haven't the faintest idea.

LEO: You're laughing inside.   You're thoroughly damned well pleased with yourself, aren't you?

OTTO: I don't know.   I don't know that either.

LEO (*savagely*): You are!   I can see it in your eyes—so much triumph—such a sweet revenge!

OTTO: It wasn't anything to do with revenge.

LEO: It was.   Of course it was—secretly thought out, planned for ages—infinitely mean!

OTTO: Shut up!   And don't talk such nonsense.

[*88*]

LEO: Why did you do it, then? Why did you come back and break everything up for me?

OTTO: I came back to see you both. It was a surprise.

LEO: A rather cruel surprise, and brilliantly successful. You should be very happy.

OTTO (*sadly*): Should I?

LEO: Perhaps I should be happy, too; you've set me free from something.

OTTO: What?

LEO (*haltingly*): The—feeling I had for you—something very deep, I imagined it was, but it couldn't have been, could it—now that it has died so easily.

OTTO: I said all that to you in Paris. Do you remember? I thought it was true then, just as you think it's true now.

LEO: It is true.

OTTO: Oh, no, it isn't.

LEO: Do you honestly believe I could ever look at you again, as a real friend?

OTTO: Until the day you die.

LEO: Shut up! It's too utterly beastly—the whole thing.

OTTO: It's certainly very, very uncomfortable.

LEO: Is Gilda going to leave me? To go away with you?

OTTO: Do you want her to?

LEO: Yes, I suppose so, now.

OTTO: We didn't make any arrangement or plans.

LEO: I came back too soon. You could have gone away and left a note for me—that would have been nice and easy for you, wouldn't it?

OTTO: Perhaps it would, really.   I don't know that I should have done it, though.

LEO: Why not?

OTTO: If I had, I shouldn't have seen you at all, and I wanted to see you very much.

LEO: You even wanted to see me, hating you like this? Very touching!

OTTO: You're not hating me nearly as much as you think you are.   You're hating the situation: that's quite different.

LEO: You flatter yourself.

OTTO: No.   I'm speaking from experience.   You forget, I've been through just what you're going through now.   I thought I hated you with all my heart and soul, and the force of that hatred swept me away onto the high seas, too far out of reach to be able to come back when I discovered the truth.

LEO: The truth!

OTTO: That no one of us was more to blame than the other.   We've made our own circumstances, you and Gilda and me, and we've bloody well got to put up with them!

LEO: I wish I could aspire to such a sublime God's-eye view!

OTTO: You will—in time—when your acids have calmed down.

LEO: I'd like so very much not to be able to feel anything at all for a little.   I'm desperately tired.

OTTO: You want a change.

LEO: It seems as if I'm going to get one, whether I want it or not.

[*90*]

OTTO (*laughing*): Oh, Leo, you really are very, very tender!

LEO: Don't laugh! How dare you laugh! How *can* you laugh!

OTTO: It's a good joke. A magnificent joke.

LEO (*bitterly*): A pity Gilda chose just that moment to go out, we could all have enjoyed it together.

OTTO: Like we did before?

LEO: Yes, like we did before.

OTTO: And like we shall again.

LEO (*vehemently*): No, *never* again—never!

OTTO: I wonder.

> *The telephone rings.* LEO *goes over mechanically to answer it; he lifts up the receiver, and as he does so he catches sight of the two letters propped up against the brandy bottle. He stares at them and slowly lets the receiver drop onto the desk.*

LEO (*very quietly*): Otto.

OTTO: What is it?

LEO: Look.

> OTTO *comes over to the desk, and they both stand staring at the letters.*

OTTO: Gilda!

LEO: Of course.

OTTO: She's gone! She's escaped!

LEO: Funny word to use, "escaped."

OTTO: That's what she's done, all the same, escaped

LEO: The joke is becoming richer.

OTTO: Escaped from both of us.

LEO: We'd better open them, I suppose.

OTTO (*slowly*): Yes—yes, I suppose we had.

> *They both open the letters, in silence, and read them.*

LEO (*after a pause*): What does yours say?

OTTO (*reading*): "Good-bye, my clever little dear! Thank you for the keys of the city."

LEO: That's what mine says.

OTTO: I wonder where she's gone?

LEO: I don't see that that matters much.

OTTO: One up to Gilda!

LEO: What does she mean, "keys of the city"?

OTTO: A lot of things.

LEO: I feel rather sick.

OTTO: Have some Sherry?

LEO: That's brandy.

OTTO: Better still.

> *He pours out a glass and hands it to* LEO.

LEO (*quietly*): Thank you.

OTTO (*pouring one out for himself*): I feel a little sick, too.

LEO: Do you think she'll come back?

OTTO: No.

LEO: She will—she must—she must come back!

OTTO: She won't.   Not for a long time.

LEO (*drinking his brandy*): It's all my fault, really.

OTTO (*drinking his*): Is it?

LEO: Yes.   I've, unfortunately, turned out to be successful.   Gilda doesn't care for successful people.

OTTO: I wonder how much we've lost, with the years?

LEO: A lot.   I think, practically everything now.

OTTO (*thoughtfully*): Love among the artists.   Very difficult, too difficult.

LEO: Do you think we could find her?

OTTO: No.

[*92*]

LEO: We could try.

OTTO: Do you want to?

LEO: Of course.

OTTO: Why?   What would be the use?

LEO: She might explain a little—a little more clearly.

OTTO: What good would that do?   We know why she's gone perfectly well.

LEO: Because she doesn't want us any more.

OTTO: Because she thinks she doesn't want us any more.

LEO: I suppose that's as good a reason as any.

OTTO: Quite.

LEO: All the same, I should like to see her just once— just to find out, really, in so many words——

OTTO (*with sudden fury*): So many words!   That's what's wrong with us!   So many words—too many words, masses and masses of words, spewed about until we're choked with them.   We've argued and probed and dragged our entrails out in front of one another for years! We've explained away the sea and the stars and life and death and our own peace of mind!   I'm sick of this endless game of three-handed, spiritual ping-pong—this battling of our little egos in one another's faces!   Sick to death of it!   Gilda's made a supreme gesture and got out. Good luck to her, I say!   Good luck to the old girl—she knows her onions!

OTTO *refills his glass and drains it at a gulp.*

LEO: You'll get drunk, swilling down all that brandy on an empty stomach.

OTTO: Why not!   What else is there to do?   Here, have some more as well.

He refills LEO's *glass and hands it to him.*

[*93*]

LEO: All right! Here goes.
He drains his glass.
Now, we start fair.
He refills both their glasses.
OTTO (*raising his glass*): Gilda! (*He drains it.*)
LEO (*doing the same*): Gilda! (*He drains it.*)
OTTO: That's better, isn't it? Much, much better.
LEO: Excellent. We shall be sick as dogs!
OTTO: Good for our livers.
LEO: Good for our immortal souls.
He refills the glasses, and raises his.
Our Immortal Souls!
OTTO (*raising his*): Our Immortal Souls!
They both drain them to the last drop.
LEO: I might have known it!
OTTO: What?
LEO: That there was going to be a break. Everything was running too smoothly, too well. I was enjoying all the small things too much.
OTTO: There's no harm in enjoying the small things.
LEO: Gilda didn't want me to.
OTTO: I know.
LEO: Did she tell you so?
OTTO: Yes, she said she was uneasy.
LEO: She might have had a little faith in me, I think. I haven't got this far just to be sidetracked by a few garlands.
OTTO: That's what I said to her; I said you wouldn't be touched, inside.
LEO: How about you?
OTTO: Catching up, Leo! Popular portraits at popular prices.

Leo: Good work or bad work?

Otto: Good. An occasional compromise, but essentials all right.

Leo (*with a glint in his eye*): Let's make the most of the whole business, shall we? Let's be photographed and interviewed and pointed at in restaurants! Let's play the game for what it's worth, secretaries and fur coats and de-luxe suites on transatlantic liners at minimum rates! Don't let's allow one shabby perquisite to slip through our fingers! It's what we dreamed many years ago and now it's within our reach. Let's cash in, Otto, and see how much we lose by it.

He refills both glasses and hands one to Otto.

Come on, my boy!

He raises his glass.

Success in twenty lessons! Each one more bitter than the last! More and better Success! Louder and funnier Success!

They both drain their glasses.

They put down their glasses, gasping slightly.

Otto (*agreeably*): It takes the breath away a bit, doesn't it?

Leo: How astonished our insides must be—all that brandy hurtling down suddenly!

Otto: On Sunday, too.

Leo: We ought to know more about our insides, Otto. We ought to know why everything does everything.

Otto: Machines! That's what we are, really—all of us! I can't help feeling a little discouraged about it every now and then.

Leo: Sheer sentimentality! You shouldn't feel discouraged at all; you should be proud.

[95]

Otto: I don't see anything to be proud about.

Leo: That's because you don't understand; because you're still chained to stale illusions. Science dispels illusions; you ought to be proud to be living in a scientific age. You ought to be proud to know that you're a minute cog in the vast process of human life.

Otto: I don't like to think I'm only a minute cog—it makes me sort of sad.

Leo: The time for dreaming is over, Otto.

Otto: Never! I'll never consent to that. Never, as long as I live! How do you know that science isn't a dream, too? A monstrous, gigantic hoax?

Leo: How could it be? It proves everything.

Otto: What does it prove? Answer me that!

Leo: Don't be silly, Otto. You must try not to be silly.

Otto (*bitterly*): A few facts, that's all. A few tawdry facts torn from the universe and dressed up in terminological abstractions!

Leo: Science is our only hope, the only hope for humanity! We've wallowed in false mysticism for centuries; we've fought and suffered and died for foolish beliefs, which science has proved to be as ephemeral as smoke. Now is the moment to open our eyes fearlessly and look at the truth!

Otto: What is the truth?

Leo (*irritably*): It's no use talking to you—you just won't try to grasp anything! You're content to go on being a romantic clod until the end of your days.

Otto (*incensed*): What about you? What about the plays you write? Turgid with romance; sodden with true love; rotten with nostalgia!

Leo (*with dignity*): There's no necessity to be rude

about my work—that's quite separate, and completely beside the point.

OTTO: Well, it oughtn't to be. It ought to be absolutely in accord with your cold, incisive, scientific viewpoint. If you're a writer it's your duty to write what you think. If you don't you're a cheat—a cheat and a hypocrite!

LEO (*loftily*): Impartial discussion is one thing, Otto. Personal bickering is another. I think you should learn to distinguish between the two.

OTTO: Let's have some more brandy.

LEO: That would be completely idiotic.

OTTO: Let's be completely idiotic!

LEO: Very well.

> *They both refill their glasses and drain them in silence.*

OTTO: There's a certain furtive delight in doing something consciously that you know perfectly well is thoroughly contemptible.

LEO: There is, indeed.

OTTO: There isn't much more left. Shall we finish it?

LEO: Certainly.

> OTTO *refills both glasses.*

OTTO (*handing* LEO *his*): Now what?

LEO: Now what what?

OTTO (*giggling slightly*): Don't keep on saying, what, what, what—it sounds ridiculous!

LEO: I wanted to know what you meant by "Now what"?

OTTO: Now what shall we drink to?

LEO (*also giggling*): Let's not drink to anything—let's just drink!

[97]

OTTO: All right.

He drinks.

LEO (*also drinking*): Beautiful!

OTTO: If Gilda came in now she'd be surprised all right, wouldn't she?

LEO: She'd be so surprised, she'd fall right over backwards!

OTTO: So should we.

They both laugh immoderately at this.

LEO (*wiping his eyes*): Oh, dear! Oh, dear, oh, dear, how silly! How very, very silly.

OTTO (*with sudden change of mood*): She'll never come back. Never.

LEO: Yes, she will—when we're very, very old, she'll suddenly come in—in a Bath chair!

OTTO (*sullenly*): Damn fool.

LEO (*with slight belligerence*): Who's a damn fool?

OTTO: You are. So am I. We both are. We were both damn fools in the first place, ever to have anything to do with her.

LEO (*admiringly*): You're awfully strong, Otto! Much, much stronger than you used to be.

OTTO: I've been all over the world; I've roughed it— that's what's made me strong. Every man ought to rough it.

LEO: That's the trouble with civilized life—it makes you soft. I've been thinking that for a long time. I've been watching myself getting softer and softer and softer —it's awful!

OTTO: You'd soon be all right if you got away from all this muck.

LEO: Yes, I know, but how?

OTTO (*putting his arm around his shoulders*): Get on a ship, Leo—never mind where it's going! Just get on a ship—a small ship.

LEO: How small?

OTTO: Very small indeed; a freighter.

LEO: Is that what you did?

OTTO: Yes.

LEO: Then I will. Where do very small ships sail from?

OTTO: Everywhere—Tilbury, Hamburg, Havre——

LEO: I'm free! I've suddenly realized it. I'm free!

OTTO: So am I.

LEO: We ought to drink to that, Otto. It's something worth drinking to. Freedom's been lost to us for a long, long time and now we've found it again! Freedom from people and things and softness! We really ought to drink to it.

OTTO: There isn't any more brandy.

LEO: What's that over there?

OTTO: Where?

LEO: On the thing.

OTTO (*going to it*): Sherry.

LEO: What's the matter with Sherry?

OTTO: All right.

    He brings over the bottle and fills their glasses.

LEO (*raising his*): Freedom!

OTTO (*doing the same*): Freedom!

    They both drink.

LEO: Very insipid.

OTTO: Tastes like brown paper.

LEO: I've never tasted brown paper.

OTTO: Neither have I.

They roar with laughter.

LEO: Sherry's a very ludicrous word, isn't it, when you begin to analyze it?

OTTO: Any word's ludicrous if you stare at it long enough.   Look at "macaroni."

LEO: That's Italian; that doesn't count.

OTTO: Well, "rigmarole" then, and "neophyte" and "haddock."

LEO: And "wimple"—wimple's the word that gets me down!

OTTO: What is a wimple?

LEO: A sort of mediæval megaphone, made of linen. Guinevere had one.

OTTO: What did she do with it?

LEO (*patiently*): Wore it, of course. What did you think she did with it?

OTTO: She might have blown down it.

LEO (*with slight irritation*): Anyhow, it doesn't matter, does it?

OTTO (*agreeably*): Not in the least.   It couldn't matter less.   I always thought Guinevere was tedious, wimple or no wimple.

LEO: I'm beginning to float a little, aren't you?

OTTO: Just leaving the ground.   Give me time!   I'm just leaving the ground——

LEO: Better have some more Sherry.

OTTO: I'm afraid it isn't very good Sherry.

LEO (*scrutinizing the bottle*): It ought to be good; it's real old Armadildo.

OTTO: Perhaps we haven't given it a fair chance.

He holds out his glass; LEO *refills it and his own.*

LEO (*raising his glass*): Après moi le déluge!

OTTO: Après both of us the deluge!

They drain their glasses.

LEO: I think I shall sit down now. I'm so terribly sick of standing up.

OTTO: Human beings were never meant to stand up, in the first place. It's all been a grave mistake.

They both sit on the sofa.

LEO: All what?

OTTO: All this stamping about.

LEO: I feel ever so much happier. I don't feel angry with you or with Gilda or with anybody! I feel sort of at peace, if you know what I mean.

OTTO (*putting his arm around him*): Yes, I know—I know.

LEO: Keys of the city, indeed!

OTTO: Lot of damned nonsense.

LEO: Too much sense of drama, flouncing off like that——

OTTO: We've all got too much sense of drama, but we won't have any more—from now onwards, reason and realism and clarity of vision.

LEO: What?

OTTO (*very loudly*): I said "Clarity of vision."

LEO: I wouldn't have believed I could ever feel like this again—so still and calm, like a deep, deep pool.

OTTO: Me, too—a deep pool, surrounded with cool green rushes, with the wind rustling through them——

This flight of fancy is disturbed by a faint hiccup.

LEO (*resting his head on* OTTO'S *shoulder*): Will you forgive me—for—for everything?

OTTO (*emotionally*): It's I who should ask you that!

LEO: I'm glad Gilda's gone, really—she was very wearisome sometimes.   I shall miss her, though.

OTTO: We shall both miss her.

LEO: She's the only really intelligent woman I've ever known.

OTTO: Brilliant!

LEO: She's done a tremendous lot for us, Otto.   I wonder how much we should have achieved without her?

OTTO: Very little, I'm afraid.   Terribly little.

LEO: And now she's gone because she doesn't want us any more.

OTTO: I think she thinks we don't want her any more.

LEO: But we do, Otto—we do——

OTTO: We shall always want her, always, always, always——

LEO (*miserably*): We shall get over it in time, I expect, but it will take years.

OTTO: I'm going to hate those years.   I'm going to hate every minute of them.

LEO: So am I.

OTTO: Thank God for each other, anyhow!

LEO: That's true.   We'll get along, somehow—(*his voice breaks*)—together——

OTTO (*struggling with his tears*): Together——

LEO (*giving way to his, and breaking down completely*): But we're going to be awfully—awfully—lonely——

   They both sob hopelessly on each other's shoulders as the curtain slowly falls.

END OF ACT TWO: SCENE 3

[*102*]

ACT THREE

Scene I

ACT THREE: Scene I

NEARLY *two years have elapsed since Act Two.*

The scene is ERNEST FRIEDMAN'S *penthouse in New York. It is an exquisite apartment, luxuriously furnished. Up stage, on the Right, are three windows opening onto a balcony. These are on an angle; below them are double doors leading into the hall. A staircase climbs up the Left-hand side of the room, leading through a curtained archway to the bedrooms, etc. Below the staircase there is a door leading to the servants' quarters.*

When the curtain rises it is about eleven-thirty on a summer night. The windows are wide open and beyond the terrace can be seen the many lights of the city. There is a table set with drinks and sandwiches, with, below it, an enormous sofa.

Voices are heard in the hall, and GILDA *enters with* GRACE TORRENCE *and* HENRY *and* HELEN CARVER. *The* CARVERS *are a comparatively young married couple, wealthy and well dressed.* GRACE TORRENCE *is slightly older, a typical Europeanized New York matron.* GILDA *is elaborately and beautifully gowned. Her manner has changed a good deal. She is much more still and sure than before. A certain amount of vitality has gone from her, but, in its place, there is an aloof poise quite in keeping with her dress and surroundings.*

[*105*]

GILDA: Who'd like a highball?

GRACE: We all would.   We all need it!

GILDA: People are wrong when they say that the opera isn't what it used to be.   It is what it used to be—that's what's wrong with it!

HENRY (*going for the drinks*): Never again!

GILDA: Is there enough ice there, Henry?

HENRY: Yes, heaps.

HELEN (*wandering out onto the terrace*): This is the most wonderful view I've ever seen!

HENRY: Next to ours.

HELEN: I like this better; you can see more of the river.

GRACE: You did all this, I suppose, Gilda?

GILDA: Not all of it; just a few extras.   Ernest laid the foundations.

GRACE: When's he coming back?

GILDA: Tomorrow.

GRACE (*wandering about the room*): It's lovely.

GILDA: I'd forgotten you hadn't been here before.

HENRY: Here, Grace.   (*He gives her a drink.*) Gilda——

GILDA (*taking one*): Thanks, Henry.

HENRY: Helen, do you want yours out there?

HELEN: No, I'll come in for it.

    She comes in, takes her drink, and sits down on the sofa.

GRACE (*stopping before an antique chair*): Where did you get this?

GILDA: Italy.   We were motoring to Siena, and we stopped at a little village for lunch and there it was—just waiting to be grabbed.

GRACE: You ought to open a shop; with your reputation you'd make a packet!

GILDA: This is my shop, really.   I make quite enough, one way and another.

HELEN: But the things in this room aren't for sale, are they?

GILDA: All except the pictures.   Those are Ernest's.

GRACE (*laughing*): Then they are for sale!

GILDA: Perhaps.   At a price.

HENRY: And, oh boy, what a price!   (*To* HELEN): What was the name of that one he sold Dad?

HELEN: I don't think it had a name.

HENRY: The name of the artist, I mean.

GILDA: Matisse.

HENRY: Well, all I can say is, it ought to have been a double Matisse for that money!

GILDA (*smiling*): Eleven thousand dollars, wasn't it?

HENRY: It was.

GILDA (*sweetly*): Your father was very lucky, but then he always has been, hasn't he?

GRACE: Bow, Henry!   Or fall down dead—one or the other!

GILDA: Do you want to see over the rest of it, Grace?

GRACE: I do, indeed!   I'm taking mental notes, and if any of them come out right, I'll send you a handsome gift.

GILDA: Terrace first?   Very nice line in balcony furniture, swing chairs, striped awnings, shrubs in pots——

GRACE: I'd rather die than go near the terrace—it makes me giddy from here.

GILDA: I love being high up.

HELEN: So do I—the higher the better!

GRACE: What floor is this?

GILDA: Thirtieth.

GRACE: I was caught by fire once on the sixth floor; I had to be hauled down a ladder in my nightgown—since then I've always lived on the ground level.

HELEN: What about burglars?

GRACE: I'd rather have fifty burglars than one fire. What would you do here if there was a fire, Gilda? If it started down below, in the elevator shaft or something?

GILDA (*pointing towards the servants' door*): Very nice line in fire escapes just through that door; perfectly equipped, commodious—there's even a wide enough balustrade to slide down.

GRACE: One day there'll be an earthquake in this city, then all you high livers will come tumbling down!

HENRY: In that case, I'd rather be here than on the ground.

GILDA: Come and see the bedrooms.

GRACE: Higher still?

GILDA: Yes, higher still. You two will be all right, won't you?

HELEN: Of course.

GILDA (*leading the way upstairs*): Help yourself to another drink, Henry.

HENRY: Thanks. I will.

GILDA *and* GRACE *disappear through the archway.*

HENRY (*at table*): Do you want another?

HELEN: I haven't finished this one yet.

HENRY: Promise me one thing, Helen?

HELEN: What?

HENRY: That you'll never become a professional decorator.

HELEN: Why?

HENRY: I've never met one yet that wasn't hard as nails, and, my God, I've met hundreds!

HELEN: Do you think Gilda's hard?

HENRY: Hard! Look at her eyes. Look at the way she's piloting old Grace round the apartment. Look at the way she snapped me up over Dad's picture!

HELEN: You were rather awful about it.

HENRY: So I should think! Eleven thousand bucks for that daub! I've only found three people who could tell me what it was supposed to be, and they all told me different.

HELEN: Art's not in your line, Henry.

HENRY: You bet your sweet life it isn't—not at that price!

HELEN: I like modern painting. I think it's thrilling.

HENRY: Bunk.

HELEN (*with superiority*): That's what everybody always says about new things. Look at Wagner.

HENRY: What's Wagner got to do with it?

HELEN: When first his music came out everyone said it was terrible.

HENRY: That's jake with me!

HELEN (*laughing patronizingly*): It's silly to laugh at things just because you don't understand them.

HENRY: You've been around too much lately, Helen; you ought to stay home more.

HELEN: If it hadn't been for Gilda, I don't know what I'd have done all winter.

HENRY: If it hadn't been for us, I don't know what she'd have done all winter! You could have fixed our apartment just as well as she did. What do we want with all that Spanish junk?

[*109*]

HELEN: It isn't junk; it's beautiful! She's got the most wonderful taste, everybody knows she has.

HENRY: It's a racket, Helen! The whole thing is a racket.

HELEN: I don't know what's the matter with you to-night.

HENRY: The evening's been a flop. The opera was lousy, and now we've been dragged up here instead of going to the Casino. Just because Gilda's sniffed a bit of business.

There is a ring at the door bell.

HELEN: Do you really think she only got Grace up here to sell her something?

HENRY: I do.

HELEN: Oh, Henry!.

HENRY: Don't you?

HELEN: No, of course I don't. They've got a lot of money; they don't need to go on like that.

HENRY: That's how they made the money. Ernest's been palming off pictures on people for years.

HELEN: I don't see why he shouldn't, if they're willing to buy them. After all, everybody sells something; I mean——

The door bell rings again.

HENRY: Don't they keep any servants?

HELEN: I expect they've gone to bed.

HENRY: I'd better answer the door, I suppose.

HELEN: Yes, I think you had.

HENRY goes off. HELEN does up her face. There is the sound of voices in the hall. HENRY reënters, followed by OTTO and LEO, both attired in very faultless evening dress.

[*110*]

HENRY: Mrs. Friedman's upstairs—I'll call her.

LEO: No, don't trouble to do that; she'll be down soon, won't she?

HENRY: Yes, she's only showing Mrs. Torrence over the apartment.

OTTO: Torrence—Torrence! How very odd! I wonder if that's the same Mrs. Torrence we met in the Yoshiwara?

LEO: Very possibly.

HENRY: This is my wife, Mrs. Carver. I'm afraid I don't know your names.

LEO: My name is Mercuré.

HELEN (*shaking hands*): How do you do, Mr. Mercuré?

OTTO: And mine is Sylvus.

HELEN (*shaking hands again*): How do you do, Mr. Sylvus?

LEO (*turning abruptly to* HENRY *and shaking his hand*): How do you do, Mr. Carver?

OTTO (*doing the same with some violence*): How do you do, Mr. Carver?

HENRY: Would you care for a drink?

LEO: Passionately.

HENRY (*coldly*): They're over there. Help yourself.

HELEN (*while they are helping themselves*): Are you old friends of Mrs. Friedman's?

OTTO (*over his shoulder*): Yes, we lived with her for years.

HELEN (*gasping slightly*): Oh!

    There is silence for a moment. OTTO *and* LEO *settle themselves comfortably in chairs.*

LEO (*raising his glass*): Here's to you, Mr. and Mrs. Carver.

OTTO (*also raising his glass*): Mr. and Mrs. Carver.

HENRY (*automatically raising his glass*): Here's luck!

There is another silence.

LEO (*conversationally*): I once knew a man called Carver in Sumatra.

HELEN: Really?

LEO: He had one of the longest beards I've ever seen.

OTTO (*quickly*): That was Mr. Eidelbaum.

LEO: So it was! How stupid of me.

OTTO (*apologetically*): We've travelled so much, you know, we sometimes get a little muddled.

HELEN (*weakly*): Yes, I expect you do.

LEO: Have you been married long?

HENRY: Two years.

LEO: Oh dear Oh dear Oh dear Oh dear Oh dear.

HENRY: Why? What of it?

OTTO: There's something strangely and deeply moving about young love, Mr. and Mrs. Carver.

LEO: Youth at the helm.

OTTO: Guiding the little fragile barque of happiness down the river of life. Unthinking, unknowing, unaware of the perils that lie in wait for you, the sudden tempests, the sharp jagged rocks beneath the surface. Are you never afraid?

HENRY: I don't see anything to be afraid of.

LEO (*fondly*): Foolish headstrong boy.

OTTO: Have you any children?

HENRY (*sharply*): No, we have not.

LEO: That's what's wrong with this century. If you were living in Renaissance Italy you'd have been married at fourteen and by now you'd have masses of children

[*112*]

and they'd be fashioning things of great beauty. Wouldn't they, Otto?

OTTO: Yes, Leo, they would.

LEO: There you are, you see!

OTTO: The tragedy of the whole situation lies in the fact that you don't care, you don't care a fig, do you?

HELEN (*stiffly*): I really don't understand what you mean.

> *Conversation again languishes.*

LEO: You've been to Chuquicamata, I suppose?

HENRY: Where?

LEO: Chuquicamata.   It's a copper mine in Chile.

HENRY: No, we haven't.   Why?

LEO (*loftily*): It doesn't matter.   It's most unimportant.

HENRY: Why do you ask?

LEO (*magnanimously*): Please don't say any more about it—it's perfectly all right.

HENRY (*with irritation*): What are you talking about?

LEO: Chuquicamata.

OTTO (*gently*): A copper mine in Chile.

HELEN (*to relieve the tension*): It's a very funny name.

> *She giggles nervously.*

LEO (*coldly*): Do you think so?

HELEN (*persevering*): Is it—is it an interesting place?

LEO: I really don't remember; I haven't been there since I was two.

OTTO: I've never been there at all.

HELEN (*subsiding*): Oh!

LEO (*after another pause*): Is Mrs. Torrence a nice woman?

HENRY: Nice!   Yes, very nice.

LEO (*with a sigh of relief*): I'm so glad.

OTTO: One can't be too careful, you know—people are so deceptive.

LEO (*grandiloquently*): It's all a question of masks, really; brittle, painted masks. We all wear them as a form of protection; modern life forces us to. We must have some means of shielding our timid, shrinking souls from the glare of civilization.

OTTO: Be careful, Leo. Remember how you upset yourself in Mombasa!

LEO: That was fish.

> HELEN *and* HENRY *exchange startled glances.* GILDA *and* GRACE *reappear through the archway and come down the stairs.* OTTO *and* LEO *and* HENRY *rise to their feet.*

GILDA (*as they come down*): . . . and the terrace is lovely in the summer, because, as it goes right round, there's always somewhere cool to sit——

> *She reaches the foot of the stairs and sees* OTTO *and* LEO. *She puts her hand onto the balustrade just for a second, to steady herself; then she speaks. Her voice is perfectly calm.*

GILDA: Hallo!

LEO: Hallo, Gilda.

OTTO: We've come back.

GILDA (*well under control*): Yes—yes, I see you have. This is Mrs. Torrence. Grace, these are two old friends of mine—Leo Mercuré and Otto Sylvus.

GRACE (*shaking hands*): Oh—how do you do.

LEO (*shaking hands*): You must forgive our clothes but we've only just come off a freight boat.

OTTO: A Dutch freight boat. The food was delicious.

GILDA: I see you both have drinks. Henry, mix me one, will you?

HENRY: Certainly.

GILDA (*in an empty voice*): This is the most delightful surprise. (*To* GRACE): Do you know, I haven't seen either of them for nearly two years.

GRACE: Gilda has been showing me this perfectly glorious apartment. Don't you think it's lovely?

OTTO (*looking around*): Artistically too careful, but professionally superb.

GILDA (*laughing lightly*): Behave yourself, Otto!

LEO: Where's darling little Ernest?

GILDA: Chicago.

HENRY: Here's your drink, Gilda.

> *He hands it to her.*

GILDA: Thank you.

GRACE (*sinking into a chair*): Where did you come from on your freight boat, Mr. Mercuré?

LEO: Manila.

OTTO: It was very hot in Manila.

LEO: It was also very hot in Singapore.

GILDA (*drily*): It always is, I believe.

OTTO: It was cooler in Hong Kong; and in Vladivostok it was downright cold!

LEO: We had to wear mittens.

HELEN: Was all this a pleasure trip?

LEO: Life is a pleasure trip, Mrs. Carver; a Cheap Excursion.

OTTO: That was very beautifully put, Leo. I shall always remember it.

> HENRY *and* HELEN's *faces set in disapproval.* GRACE *looks slightly bewildered.*

[*115*]

GRACE (*with a little social laugh*): Well, life certainly hasn't been a cheap excursion for me! Every day it gets more and more expensive. Everyone here has had the most dreadful winter. I was in Europe, of course, but they were feeling it there, too, very badly. Paris, particularly. Paris seemed to have lost its vitality; it used to be much more gay, somehow——

OTTO: I once had a flat in Paris. It was really more a studio than a flat, but I had to leave it.

GRACE: They pulled it down, I suppose. They're pulling down everything in Paris, now.

OTTO: They pulled it down to the ground; it was a small edifice and crumbled easily.

GRACE: It's sad, isn't it, to think of places where one has lived not being there any more?

LEO: I remember a friend of mine called Mrs. Purdy being very upset once when her house in Dorset fell into the sea.

GRACE (*startled*): How terrible!

LEO: Fortunately Mr. Purdy happened to be in it at the time.

OTTO: In my case, of course, it was more like an earthquake than anything else, a small but thorough earthquake with the room trembling and the chandelier swinging and the ground opening at my feet.

GRACE: Funny. We were talking about earthquakes just now.

LEO: I've never been able to understand why the Japanese are such a cheerful race. All that hissing and grinning on the brink of destruction.

OTTO: The Japanese don't mind destruction a bit; they like it, it's part of their upbringing. They're

[*116*]

delighted with death. Look at the way they kill themselves on the most whimsical of pretexts.

LEO: I always thought Madame Butterfly was overhasty.

OTTO: She should have gone out into the world and achieved an austere independence. Just like you, Gilda.

GILDA: Don't talk nonsense. (*To* GRACE): They both talk the most absurd nonsense; they always have, ever since I've known them. You mustn't pay any attention to them.

OTTO: Don't undermine our social poise, Gilda, you— who have so much!

GILDA (*sharply*): Your social poise is nonexistent.

LEO: We have a veneer, though; it's taken us years to acquire; don't scratch it with your sharp witty nails— *darling!*

> *Everybody jumps slightly at the word "darling."*

GILDA: Have you written any new plays, Leo? Have you painted any new pictures, Otto? You must both come to lunch one day and tell me all about yourselves.

LEO: That would be delightful. Just the three of us.

OTTO: Should old acquaintance be forgot.

LEO: Close harmony.

GILDA: You'll have to forgive me if I'm not quite as helpful to you as I used to be. My critical faculties aren't as strong as they once were. I've grown away, you see.

LEO: How far have you grown away, my dear love? How lonely are you in your little box so high above the arena? Don't you ever feel that you want to come down in the cheap seats again, nearer to the blood and the sand and the warm smells, nearer to Life and Death?

[*117*]

GILDA: You've changed, Leo. You used to be more subtle.

OTTO: You've changed, too, but we expected that.

HELEN (*social poise well to the fore*): It's funny how people alter; only the other day in the Colony a boy that I used to know when he was at Yale walked up to my table, and I didn't recognize him!

LEO: Just fancy!

OTTO: Do you know, I have an excellent memory for names, but I cannot for the life of me remember faces. Sometimes I look at Leo suddenly and haven't the faintest idea who he is.

LEO (*quickly*): I can remember *things*, though, very clearly, and past conversations and small trivial incidents. Some trick of the light, some slight movement, can cause a whole flock of irrelevant memories to tumble into my mind—just unattached fragments, which might have been significant once but which don't seem to mean anything any more. Trees in a quiet London square, for instance—a green evening dress, with earrings to match—two notes propped up against a brandy bottle—odd, isn't it?

GILDA: Not particularly odd. The usual litter of an oversentimental mind.

OTTO: Be careful, Gilda. An ugly brawl is imminent.

GILDA: I'm not afraid.

OTTO: That's brave, when you have so much to lose.
    He glances comprehensively round the room.

GILDA (*quietly*): Is that a threat?

OTTO: We've come back. That should be threat enough!

GILDA (*rising, with a strange smile*): There now!

That's what happens when ghosts get into the house. They try to frighten you with their beckoning fingers and clanking chains, not knowing that they're dead and unable to harm you any more.   That's why one should never be scared of them, only sorry for them.   Poor little ghosts! It must be so uncomfortable, wandering through empty passages, feeling they're not wanted very much.

LEO (*to* GRACE): You see, Gilda can talk nonsense too.

OTTO (*reprovingly*): That wasn't nonsense, Leo; that was a flight of fancy, tinged with the macabre and reeking with allegory—a truly remarkable achievement!

LEO: It certainly requires a vivid imagination to describe this apartment as an empty passage.

GILDA (*laughing a trifle wildly*): Stop it, both of you! You're behaving abominably!

OTTO: We're all behaving abominably.

LEO: The veneer is wearing thin.   Even yours, Gilda.

GRACE: This, really, is the most extraordinary conversation I've ever heard.

OTTO: Fascinating, though, don't you think?   Fascinating to lift the roofs a fraction and look down into the houses.

GILDA: Not when the people inside know you're looking: not when they're acting for you and strutting about and showing off!

LEO: How does it feel to be so secure, Gilda?   Tell us about it?

GILDA (*ignoring him*): Another drink, Henry?

HENRY: No, thanks.

HELEN (*rising*): We really ought to be going now.

GILDA: Oh, I'm so sorry!

[*119*]

LEO: Watch the smooth wheels going round!

OTTO: Reach for a Murad!

GRACE (*also rising*): I'm going, too, Gilda. Can I drop anybody?

HENRY: No, thanks, our car's outside.

GRACE: Good-night, Mr. Mercuré.

LEO (*shaking hands*): Good-night.

GRACE (*shaking hands with* OTTO): Good-night. Can I drop you anywhere?

OTTO: No, thank you; we're staying a little longer.

GILDA: No! Go now, Otto, please. Both of you, go with Grace. I'm terribly tired; you can telephone me first thing in the morning.

LEO: We want to talk to you.

GILDA: Tomorrow, you can talk to me tomorrow; we can all talk for hours.

LEO: We want to talk now.

GILDA: I know you do, but I tell you, I'm tired—dreadfully tired. I've had a very hard day——

>   *She winks at them violently.*

OTTO (*grinning*): Oh, I see.

HELEN (*at the door*): Come on, Henry! Good-night, Gilda darling; it's been a lovely evening.

>   *She bows to* OTTO *and* LEO, *and goes out.* GRACE *looks at* OTTO *and* LEO *and* GILDA, *and then with great tact joins* HENRY *at the door.*

GRACE (*to* OTTO): My car's there, if you are coming now. Good-night, Gilda—ring for the elevator, Henry——

>   *She goes out with* HENRY.

GILDA (*hurriedly, in a whisper*): It was awful of you to behave like that! Why couldn't you have waited quietly until they'd gone?

[*120*]

LEO (*also in a whisper*): They wouldn't go—they were going to stay for ever and ever and ever!

GILDA *runs over to her bag, which is lying on a chair, and takes a latchkey out of it.*

GILDA: Go, now, both of you!   Go with Grace.   She'll gossip all over the town if you don't.   Here's the key; come back in ten minutes.

OTTO: Intrigue, eh?   A nice state of affairs.

LEO: Good old Decameron!

GILDA (*shoving the key into his hand*): Go on, quickly! Get a taxi straight back——

They both kiss her lightly on the lips and go out.

GILDA *stands still, staring after them until she hears the door slam.   Her eyes are filled with tears.   She strides about the room in great agitation, clasping and unclasping her hands.   She stops in front of a table on which is someone's unfinished drink.   She drinks it thoughtfully, frowning and tapping her foot nervously on the ground.*

Suddenly, she bangs down the glass, snatches up her cloak and bag, switches off all the lights, and runs out through the door leading to the fire escape.

Curtain.

END OF ACT THREE: SCENE I

ACT THREE

Scene II

ACT THREE: Scene II

THE SCENE *is the same, and it is the next morning.*

The windows are wide open, and sunlight is streaming into the room.

As the curtain rises, MATTHEW *crosses over from the servants' quarters, door Left, and goes into the hall.* MATTHEW *is black but comely. He wears a snow-white coat and dark trousers and is very smart indeed.*

ERNEST *enters from the hall, carrying a suitcase.*

MATTHEW *follows him, staggering under three or four large canvases in a wooden crate.*

ERNEST: Put them down there for the moment, Matthew, and get me some coffee.

MATTHEW: Yes, sir.

He rests the canvases against the wall.

ERNEST (*taking off his hat and coat*): Is Mrs. Friedman awake?

MATTHEW: She hasn't rung yet, sir.

ERNEST: All right. Get me the coffee as quickly as you can.

MATTHEW: It's all ready, sir.

He goes off Left. ERNEST *wanders out onto the terrace and then in again. He picks up a newspaper off the table, glances at it and throws it down again. He is obviously irritable.* MATTHEW *reënters with a breakfast tray, which he places on a small table.*

[*125*]

MATTHEW: Perhaps you'd like to have it out on the terrace, sir?

ERNEST: No. This'll do.

MATTHEW: Did you have a good trip, sir?

ERNEST (*sitting down at the table*): No, I did not.

MATTHEW: Very good, sir.

> *He goes out.* ERNEST *pours himself some coffee. While he is doing so,* OTTO *and* LEO *come down the stairs. They are both wearing* ERNEST'S *pyjamas and dressing gowns, which are considerably small for them. Their feet are bare.*

LEO (*as they reach the bottom of the stairs*): Good-morning, Ernest!

ERNEST (*flabbergasted*): God bless my soul!

OTTO (*kissing him*): He will, Ernest. He couldn't fail to!

LEO (*also kissing him*): Dear little Ernest!

ERNEST: Where—where in heaven's name have you come from?

OTTO: Manila.

LEO (*grinning*): It was very hot in Manila.

OTTO: Aren't you pleased to see us?

ERNEST: Have you been staying here?

LEO: Of course.

ERNEST: Since when?

OTTO: Last night.

ERNEST: Where did you sleep?

LEO: Upstairs.

ERNEST: What! Where's Gilda?

OTTO: We don't know. She's disappeared.

ERNEST: Disappeared! What on earth do you mean?

OTTO: What I say. She's disappeared.

[*126*]

Leo: Disappeared!   Gone. She fluttered out into the night like a silly great owl.

Otto: We arrived when she was entertaining a few smart friends, and she pressed a latchkey into our hands and told us to come back later; and when we came back later, she wasn't here.   So we waited a little while, and then we went to bed.

Leo: We were very tired.

Ernest: It's fantastic, the whole thing!   Ridiculous.

Leo: Do you think we could have some coffee?

Ernest: Yes, you can have some coffee, if you want it.

> *He rings a little bell on the table and slams it down again irritably.*

Otto: I do hope you're not going to be disagreeable, Ernest.   After all, you haven't seen us for ages.

Ernest: Disagreeable!   What do you expect me to be?   I arrive home after twenty hours in the train to find Gilda gone, and you both staying in the house uninvited and wearing my pyjamas.

Leo: We'll take them off at once, if you like.

Ernest: You won't do any such thing!

> Matthew *enters and stands stricken with astonishment.*

Two more cups, Matthew.

Matthew: Yes, sir.

> *He goes out, staring.*

Ernest: Had you warned Gilda that you were coming?

Otto: No. We just arrived—it was a surprise.

Ernest (*suddenly*): What do you want?

Leo: Why do you ask that?

[*127*]

ERNEST: I want to know. Why have you come? What do you want?

OTTO: We want Gilda, of course!

ERNEST: Have you gone out of your mind?

LEO: Not at all. It's quite natural. We've always wanted Gilda.

ERNEST: Are you aware that she is my wife?

OTTO (*turning away*): Oh, don't be so silly, Ernest!

ERNEST: Silly! How dare you!

LEO: You're a dear old pet, Ernest, and we're very, very fond of you and we know perfectly well that Gilda could be married to you fifty times and still not be your wife.

MATTHEW *comes in with two cups.*

MATTHEW: Do you want some fresh coffee, sir?

ERNEST (*mechanically, staring at them*): No—no, there's enough here.

MATTHEW (*to* OTTO): Can I get you some grapefruit, sir? Or an egg?

OTTO: No, thank you.

MATTHEW (*to* LEO): For you, sir?

LEO: No, thank you.

ERNEST: That will do, Matthew.

MATTHEW: Yes, sir.

He goes out.

ERNEST: Do you seriously imagine that you have the slightest right to walk into my house like this and demand my wife?

OTTO: Do stop saying "my wife" in that complacent way, Ernest; it's absurd!

LEO: We know entirely why you married Gilda; and if

[*128*]

we'd both been dead it would have been an exceedingly good arrangement.

ERNEST: You are dead, as far as she's concerned.

OTTO: Oh, no, we're not! We're very much alive.

LEO: I fear your marriage is on the rocks, Ernest.

ERNEST: This is one of the most superb exhibitions of brazen impertinence I've ever encountered.

OTTO: It's inconvenient, I do see that. It may quite possibly inconvenience you very much.

LEO: But no more than that; and you know it as well as we do.

ERNEST (*with admirable control*): Aren't you taking rather a lot for granted?

OTTO: Only what we know.

ERNEST: I won't lose my temper with you, because that would be foolish——

OTTO: And ineffective.

ERNEST: But I think you had better put on whatever clothes you came in, and go away. You can come back later, when you're in a more reasonable frame of mind.

LEO: We're in a perfectly reasonable frame of mind, Ernest. We've never been more reasonable in our lives; nor more serenely determined.

ERNEST (*with great calmness*): Now look here, you two. I married Gilda because she was alone, and because for many, many years I have been deeply attached to her. We discussed it carefully together from every angle, before we decided. I know the whole circumstances intimately. I know exactly how much she loved you both; and also, I'm afraid, exactly how little you both loved her. You practically ruined her life between you, and you caused her great unhappiness with your egotisti-

[*129*]

cal, casual passions. Now you can leave her alone. She's worked hard and made a reputation for herself. Her life is fully occupied; and she is completely contented. Leave her alone! Go away! Go back to Manila or wherever you came from—and leave her alone!

LEO: Admirable, Ernest! Admirable, but not strictly accurate. We love her more than anyone else in the world and always shall. She caused us just as much unhappiness in the past as we ever caused her. And although she may have worked hard, and although her life is so fully occupied, she is far from being contented. We saw her last night and we know.

OTTO: She could never be contented without us, because she belongs to us just as much as we belong to her.

ERNEST: She ran away from you.

LEO: She'll come back.

The front door bell rings.

OTTO: She has come back!

There is silence while MATTHEW *crosses from the servants' door to the hall.*

LEO: Coffee! That's the thing—nice, strong coffee!

He pours some out for himself.

OTTO (*doing the same*): Delicious!

ERNEST (*rising, and flinging down his napkin*): This is insupportable!

LEO: Peculiar and complicated, I grant you, and rather exciting, but not insupportable.

GILDA *enters, followed by* MATTHEW, *who looks utterly bewildered. She is wearing a dark day coat and hat over her evening dress, and carrying a brown paper parcel that is obviously her evening cloak. She sees the three of them and smiles.*

[*130*]

GILDA: I might have known it!

MATTHEW: Shall I take your parcel, ma'am?

GILDA: Yes, give it to Nora, Matthew; it's my evening cloak.

MATTHEW: Yes, ma'am.

He goes off, Left, with it; while GILDA *takes off her hat and coat and fluffs out her hair.*

GILDA: I borrowed this coat and hat from the telephone operator at the Ritz: remind me to return it some time this morning, Ernest.

She comes over and kisses him absently.

This is all very awkward, isn't it? I am so sorry. The very first minute you get home, too. It's a shame! (*To* OTTO *and* LEO): Did you stay here all night?

LEO: Yes, we did.

GILDA: I wondered if you would.

OTTO: Why did you sneak off like that?

GILDA (*coolly*): I should have thought the reason was obvious enough.

LEO: It was very weak of you.

GILDA: Not at all. I wanted time to think. Give me some coffee, Ernest—no, don't ring for another cup; I'll have yours. I couldn't bear to see Matthew's eyes popping out at me any more!

She pours out some coffee and sits down and surveys the three of them.

GILDA (*blandly*): Now then!

LEO: Now then *indeed!*

GILDA: What's going to happen?

OTTO: Social poise again. Oh, dear! Oh, dear, oh, dear!

GILDA: You know you both look figures of fun in those pyjamas!

ERNEST: I don't believe I've ever been so acutely irritated in my whole life.

LEO: It is annoying for you, Ernest, I do see that! I'm so sorry.

OTTO: Yes, we're both sorry.

ERNEST: I think your arrogance is insufferable. I don't know what to say. I don't know what to do. I'm very, very angry. Gilda, for heaven's sake, tell them to go!

GILDA: They wouldn't.   Not if I told them until I was black in the face!

LEO: Quite right.

OTTO: Not without you, we wouldn't.

GILDA (*smiling*): That's very sweet of you both.

LEO (*looking at her sharply*): What are you up to?

OTTO: Tell us, my little dear, my clever little dear! Tell us what you're up to.

GILDA: What have you been saying to Ernest?

LEO: Lots of things.

ERNEST: They've been extremely offensive, both of them.

GILDA: In what way?

ERNEST: I'd rather not discuss it any further.

GILDA: I believe you've got a little fatter, Otto.

LEO: He eats too much rice.

GILDA: You look very well, though.

OTTO (*raising his eyebrows slightly*): Thank you.

GILDA: So do you, Leo.   The line in between your eyes is deeper, but you seem very healthy.

LEO: I am.

GILDA: You were always very strong, constitutionally. Strong as an ox!   Do you remember that, Ernest?

[*132*]

Ernest (*irritably*): What?

Gilda (*smiling*): Nothing. It doesn't matter.

Leo: Stop pulling our ears and stroking us, Gilda, and tell us your secret. Tell us why you're so strange and quiet—tell us what you're up to.

Gilda: Don't you know? I've given in!

Leo (*quickly*): What!

Gilda (*quietly and very distinctly*): I've given in. I've thrown my hand in! The game's over.

Ernest: Gilda! What do you mean?

Gilda: What I say.

Ernest: You mean—you can't mean that——

Gilda (*gently*): I mean I'm going away from you, Ernest. Some things are too strong to fight against; I've been fighting for two years and it's no use. I'm bored with the battle, sick to death of it! So I've given in.

Ernest: You're—you're insane! You can't be serious.

Gilda: I'm not serious! That's what's so dreadful. I feel I ought to be but I'm not—my heart's bobbing up and down inside me like a parrot in a cage! It's shameful, I know, but I can't help it—— (*She suddenly turns on* Otto *and* Leo): And you two—you two sitting there with the light of triumph in your eyes!—Say something, can't you! Say something, for God's sake, before I slap your smug little faces!

Leo: I knew it. I knew it last night!

Otto: We both knew it! We laughed ourselves to sleep.

Ernest: Gilda, pull yourself together! Don't be a fool—pull yourself together!

Gilda: Don't get excited, Ernest. It doesn't matter to you as much as all that, you know.

[*133*]

ERNEST: You're crazy! You're stark staring mad!

GILDA (*ecstatically*): I am, I am! I'm mad with joy! I'm mad with relief! I thought they really had forgotten me; that they really were free of me. I thought that they were never coming back, that I should never see them again; that my heart would be heavy and sick and lonely for them until I died!

LEO: Serve you right for leaving us! Serve you damn well right!

GILDA: Be quiet! Shut your trap, my darling! I've got to explain to Ernest.

ERNEST: I don't want to hear your explanations. I don't want to hear any more——

OTTO: Try and stop her, that's all! Just try and stop her! She's off, she's embarked on a scene. Oh, dear love, this is highly delectable! The old girl's on the war path!

GILDA: Be quiet, I tell you! Don't crow! Don't be so mean.

ERNEST: I don't want to hear any more, I tell you!

GILDA: You've got to. You must! There's so much I have to say. You must listen. In fairness to yourself and to all of us, you must listen.

ERNEST: You're being unbelievably vulgar! I'm ashamed of you.

GILDA: I'm ashamed of many things, but not of this! This is real. I've made use of you, Ernest, and I'm ashamed of that, and I've lied to you. I'm ashamed of that, too; but at least I didn't know it: I was too busy lying to myself at the same time. I took refuge in your gentle, kind friendship, and tried to pretend to myself that it was enough, but it wasn't. I've talked and laughed and entertained your friends; I've been excellent company and very efficient. I've worked hard and bought things and sold things, all the time pretending that my longing for these two was fading! But it wasn't. They came back last night, looking very sleek and sly in their newly pressed suits, and the moment I saw them, I knew; I knew it was no good pretending any more. I fought against it, honestly I did! I ran away from them, and walked about the streets and sat in Childs weeping into glasses of milk. Oh, Ernest, you've understood such a lot, understand just this much more, and try to forgive me—because I can't possibly live without them, and that's that!

ERNEST (*with icy calm*): I gather that the fact that I'm your husband is not of the faintest importance to you?

GILDA: It's never been anything more than a comfortable sort of arrangement, has it?

ERNEST: Apparently not as comfortable as I imagined.

GILDA: Exquisitely comfortable, Ernest, and easygoing and very, very nice; but those things don't count in a situation like this, you must see that!

ERNEST: I see a ruthless egotism, an utter disregard for anyone's feelings but your own. That's all I can see at the moment.

LEO: You should see more, Ernest, you really should. The years that you've known us should have taught you that it's no use trying to make any one of us toe the line for long.

ERNEST: Gilda is different from you two, she always has been.

GILDA: Not different enough.

ERNEST: You let her down utterly. You threw away

[*135*]

everything she gave you. It was painful to watch her writhing in the throes of her own foolish love for you. I used to love you both too. You were young and gay, and your assurance wasn't set and unbecoming as it is now. But I don't love you any more. I'm not even fond of you. You set every instinct that I have on edge. You offend my taste. When Gilda escaped from you I tried to make her happy and contented, quietly, without fuss.

OTTO: She could never be happy without fuss. She revels in it.

ERNEST: Superficially, perhaps, but not really. Not deep down in her heart.

LEO: What do you know of her heart?

GILDA: Cruel little cat.

OTTO: Shut up!

LEO: She's chosen to come back to us. She just said so. How do you account for that?

ERNEST: The sight of you has revived her old idiotic infatuation for you, but only for a little. It won't last. She knows too much now to be taken in by you again.

GILDA: You're wrong, Ernest. You're wrong.

ERNEST: Your lack of balance verges on insanity.

OTTO: Do you know that was downright rude!

GILDA: Why go on talking? Talking isn't any good. Look at me, Ernest. Look at me! Can't you see what's happened?

ERNEST: You're a mad woman again.

GILDA: Why shouldn't I be a mad woman? I've been sane and still for two years. You were deceived by my dead behaviour because you wanted to be. It's silly to go on saying to yourself that I'm different from Otto and Leo just because you want to believe it. I'm not different from them. We're all of a piece, the three of us. Those early years made us so. From now on we shall have to live and die our own way. No one else's way is any good, we don't fit.

ERNEST: No, you don't, you don't and you never will. Your values are false and distorted.

GILDA: Only from your point of view.

ERNEST: From the point of view of anyone who has the slightest sense of decency.

LEO: We have our own decencies. We have our own ethics. Our lives are a different shape from yours. Wave us good-bye, Little Ernest, we're together again.

GILDA: Ernest, Ernest, be friendly. It can't hurt you much.

ERNEST: Not any more. I've wasted too much friendship on all of you, you're not worth it.

OTTO: There's a lot of vanity in your anger, Ernest, which isn't really worthy of your intelligence.

ERNEST (*turning on him*): Don't speak to me, please!

LEO: Otto's perfectly right. This behaviour isn't worthy of your intelligence. If you were twisted up inside and really unhappy it would be different; but you're not, you're no more than offended and resentful that your smooth habits should be tampered with——

ERNEST (*losing control*): Hold your tongue!—I've had too much of your effrontery already!

GILDA (*peaceably*): Once and for all, Ernest, don't be bitter and so dreadfully outraged! Please, please calm down and you'll find it much easier to understand.

ERNEST: You overrate my capacity for understanding! I don't understand; the whole situation is revolting to me.

I never shall understand; I never could understand this disgusting three-sided erotic hotch-potch!

GILDA: Ernest!

LEO: Why, good heavens! King Solomon had a hundred wives and was thought very highly of. I can't see why Gilda shouldn't be allowed a couple of gentlemen friends.

ERNEST (*furiously*): Your ill-timed flippancy is only in keeping with the rest of your execrable taste!

OTTO: Certain emotions transcend even taste, Ernest. Take anger, for example. Look what anger's doing to you! You're blowing yourself out like a frog!

ERNEST (*beside himself*): Be quiet! Be quiet!

LEO (*violently*): Why should we be quiet! You're making enough row to blast the roof off! Why should you have the monopoly of noise? Why should your pompous moral pretensions be allowed to hurtle across the city without any competition? We've all got lungs; let's use them! Let's shriek like mad! Let's enjoy ourselves!

GILDA (*beginning to laugh*): Stop it, Leo! I implore you!—This is ludicrous! Stop it—stop it——

ERNEST (*in a frenzy*): It is ludicrous! It's ludicrous to think that I was ever taken in by any of you—that I ever mistook you for anything but the unscrupulous, worthless degenerates that you are! There isn't a decent instinct among the lot of you. You're shifty and irresponsible and abominable, and I don't wish to set eyes on you again—as long as I live! Never! Do you hear me? Never—never—never!

> *He stamps out of the room, quite beside himself with fury; on his way into the hall he falls over the package of canvases.*

[*138*]

This is too much for GILDA *and* OTTO *and* LEO; *they break down utterly and roar with laughter. They groan and weep with laughter; their laughter is still echoing from the walls as—*

THE CURTAIN FALLS

[*139*]

CPSIA information can be obtained at www.ICGtesting.com
Printed in the USA
LVOW041624060312

271867LV00008B/152/A